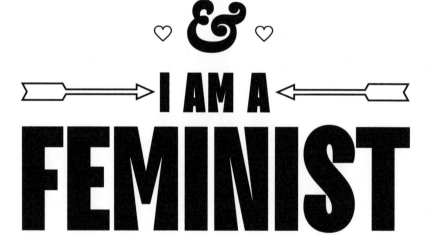

I LOVE ROMCOMS & I AM A FEMINIST

I LOVE ROMCOMS

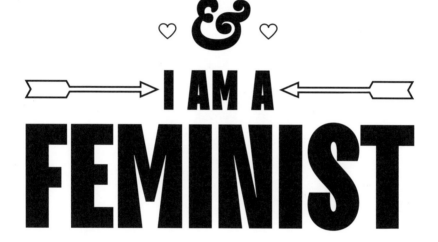

& I AM A FEMINIST

A Manifesto in **100** Romcoms

CORRINA ANTROBUS

Illustrated by Vulga Drawings

WHITE LION
PUBLISHING

★★★ CONTENTS

THE ROMCOM THAT...

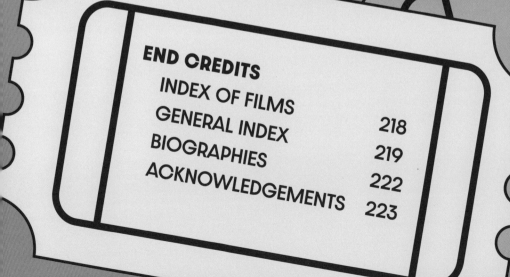

DEAR FEMINIST ROMCOM LOVER,

I know. For years you've had to file your enjoyment away as a 'guilty' pleasure or turn a blushing blind eye to the apparent misogyny that lingers within such a pink and fluffy genre. But enough. Allow this book to defend your taste from ridicule, strengthen your weakness for romance and sophisticate your knowledge of films that you didn't even realize were romantic comedies (because they were probably too embarrassed to admit it themselves).

Across the 100 romcoms – and, to broaden the qualification of some of these titles, 'chick flicks' – in this book, lies an eclectic mix of films that have contributed to the advancement of female representation or hauled the genre up from a steaming gutter of sexism. Prepare to relish the underdogs of the romcom world and let us not spend any more time debating the divisive charms of Woody Allen and John Hughes or trying to decide if *Love Actually* is just a 136-minute insult. Herein lie women who have exercised power, lampooned societal expectations and added complexity to the female experience – and within a genre that's charged with habitually undermining women, these wins are all the more triumphant.

Let's face it: society has long treated things that target women as banal. Even breaking apart the words 'chick' and 'flick' is an admission of how lowly we're prepared to label both women and art that is so resolutely aligned to femininity. And it's demeaning to think how the only genre that routinely centres the lives of women suffers from being dismissed as derogative fluff, especially when beloved romcom writers Nora Ephron, Terry McMillan, Nia Vardalos and Nancy Meyers were so generously autobiographical in their work. And while visionary male filmmakers Wes Anderson, Yorgos Lanthimos and Tim Burton are hailed for their meticulous set design, the punctilious interior house porn of Nancy Meyers is rarely appreciated as a craft.

Further dismissal may also lie in the unfavourable critics' response, which is unsurprising given the sector has long been dominated by men. Before you say, 'Not all men!' – you're right. Not all men. Despite the 38 per cent Rotten Tomato critic score that *Maid in Manhattan* (see page 112) received, discerning critic Roger Ebert lauded the film as 'skilful', while reminding us to lean into the fantasy in order to enjoy the fun, saying, 'We go to

HEREIN LIE WOMEN WHO HAVE EXERCISED POWER...

the movies for many reasons, and one of them is to see attractive people fall in love. This is not shameful. It is alright to go to a romantic comedy and not demand it be a searing portrait of the way we live now.'

While Ebert highlights that denouncing romcoms for their lack of realism further smacks of sexism (can't a girl dream?), in fact, the best romantic comedies reflect the feminism of their time. From the Suffragette spirit of Zona Gale's 1921 *Miss Lulu Bett* (see page 16), through to Greta Gerwig's 2023 *Barbie* (see page 214) challenging toxic gender norms, many of these films are products of misogynist exhaustion and signal a snapping point for inadequate representation. See *Boy Meets Girl* (see page 158), which welcomed trans women's bodies into the mix; Gillian Robespierre's *Obvious Child* (see page 160), which was hailed as the first 'abortion romcom'; and Cheryl Dunye's *The Watermelon Woman* (see page 72), which earnestly asked, 'Why do Black women's stories never get told?' And as the Eighties saw more women enter the workforce, *Baby Boom* (see page 42), *Broadcast News* (see page 44) and *Working Girl* (see page 52)

saw female characters fall more in love with their career than a man.

To further the nonsensical accusations, many blame romcoms for breeding unrealistic expectations of love, which is as patronizing as thinking romcom lovers still believe in Santa. Why not just pat us on the head and tell us to settle for less? Besides, watching romcoms with your partner can be good for your marriage: in 2014, after surveying 174 newlyweds who had been made to watch and discuss five romcoms a month, the University of Rochester, USA, reported the divorce rate had halved. Actor/writer Mindy Kaling has also addressed the preposterousness of assuming romcom lovers are naive. For the *New Yorker* she wrote, 'I regard romantic comedies as a subgenre of sci-fi, in which the world operates according to different rules than my regular human world. For me, there is no difference between Ripley from *Alien* and any Katherine Heigl character. They are equally implausible,' before concluding, 'I enjoy every second of it.'

But let's not get too pernickety about genre, for it is just a label to help movies

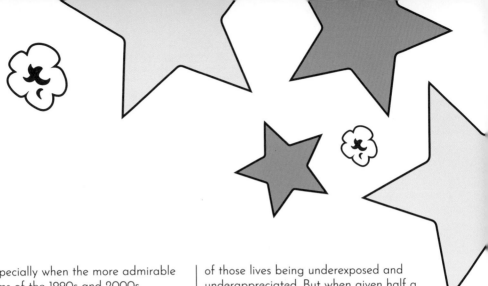

sell. Especially when the more admirable romcoms of the 1990s and 2000s (*Boomerang*, see page 58; *Love Jones*, see page 74; *Love & Basketball*, see page 94 and *Brown Sugar*, see page 110) were monolithically classed as 'Black films', meaning they got completely overlooked. As for Bollywood movies, who have long appreciated the sweet cinematic elixir of love, humour and song to huge financial success, they've also been exoticized in a ghetto of their own.

Instead, appreciate that these 100 films relish both love and laughter, and have done their bit to remind us that that's what life's about – for as long as we're all falling in and out of love, the romcom will always be an outlet for catharsis and joy. And it's time we kissed goodbye to the singular notion of romance, when our most enduring loves are often with our friends. As for thinking that only straight white people fall in love, let this book prove that wrong, while considering the humanitarian power of watching people fall in love. While we're weirdly fascinated with who's sleeping with whom, ignorance has spawned racism, transphobia and homophobia, after years

of those lives being underexposed and underappreciated. But when given half a chance, romantic comedies humanize all shapes of love, while keeping the subject buoyed on an accessible dinghy of laughs.

Thankfully, those chances to depict an inclusive range of relationships have slowly seen a rise and it's fair to say this renaissance is down to romcoms becoming diverse. As, come 2015, when Netflix moved into film-making, storytellers systematically shunned from Hollywood were stepping out of the shade. Since then, the 2017 festival hit *The Incredible Jessica James* (see page 176), 2018's acclaimed *Set It Up* (see page 182) and *To All the Boys I've Loved Before* (see page 184), all with female writers and directors and interracial romances, gave romcoms relatability and integrity – and gave us less reason to cringe. And it's been a relief to see the trend fluttering back into cinemas with the likes of *What's Love Got to Do with It?* (see page 210) and *Rye Lane* (see page 212) making hearts go weak.

As for saying romantic comedies are cliché, that's a cliché in itself. People don't

ROMCOMS WILL ALWAYS BE AN OUTLET FOR JOY

trash war films because they know who won the battle. Of course, how we get to the happily ever after shouldn't be completely trite, so while many of these titles have a familiar final destination, the route is spiced up with real-world obstacles that overwhelmingly tend to affect women. Anyway, there's something to be said about the healing powers of familiarity, especially in troubling times. Is it any wonder forgotten gems such as *Moonstruck* (see page 46) and *Down with Love* (see page 116) (or any classic romcoms, period) saw a revival in the 2020 pandemic?

This 2020s resurgence has been steadily on the rise, proving the assumed 'death of the romcom' was all but a blip. Just look at the $200m box-office figure of *Anyone But You* (the first R-rated romcom to surpass such numbers since 2016's *Bridget Jones's Baby*), and Aline Brosh McKenna's *Your Place or Mine* – the sixth-most-watched movie on Netflix in 2023. To be fair the romcom never really died, it just took a vacation to TV. While popular series *Jane the Virgin, Insecure, High Fidelity* and *The Mindy Project* kept its seat warm, they also paved the way for 2024's *One Day, Mr & Mrs Smith* and Lena Dunham's anticipated comeback *Too Much*. It all goes to show, like any long-term relationship, you've got to find new ways to keep the magic alive. And as we creep into

a world with a more inclusive conscience, there's faith that the romcom will evolve with a more roomy heart.

When done right, the romcom always has female solidarity at play and often that kinship transcends to compassion towards the real-life experiences of the women involved. Take *Notting Hill* (see page 86), *Maid in Manhattan* and *The Break Up's* (see page 126) meta winks to how their leading women were viciously hounded by the press. Or how *Boomerang's* 'controversial' casting of Robin Givens proved she was more than a 'gold digger' for reporting her then husband Mike Tyson for spousal abuse. But also watch *Waitress* (see page 130), in loving memory of its writer/director Adrienne Shelly, who was tragically murdered just before her film was released. *Waitress* then went on to become a hit Broadway musical and became the first of its kind to be driven by an all-female team.

So, let's look at romantic comedies with new rose-tinted eyes using these 100 superior examples to prove they're smarter than they look. Each one does its bit to triumph over a societal pressure – and with many of these challenges lying within the expectations of relationships (from how quickly we have sex, to whether we work after marriage), let's appreciate the romcom as a fun way to protest.

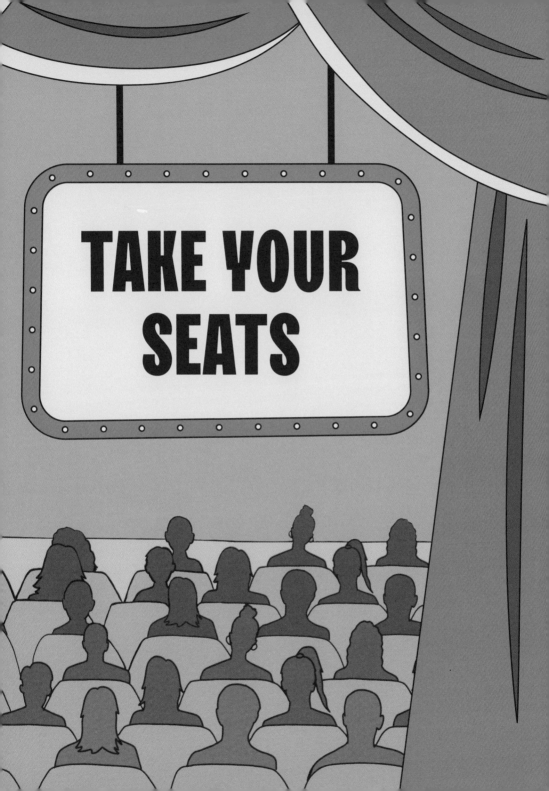

GAVE WOMEN AN EARLY LESSON IN SELF-RESPECT

MISS LULU BETT

DIRECTOR: William C. de Mille
WRITERS: Zona Gale, Clara Beranger
YEAR: 1921

Ever since we began blending comedy and romance, romcoms have reflected the feminism of the time. Granted, this feminism is often muddied in the waters where a disproportionate amount of men have overwhelmed the film-making space. It's why we need to look to romcoms told authentically from a woman's perspective (which doesn't rule out men who put in the work), since here is where our experiences gleam with sincerity and heart, as demonstrated in this silent-film gem.

Miss Lulu Bett is the bestselling 1920 novel that saw Zona Gale become the first woman to win a Pulitzer Prize for the play adaptation in 1921. Unmarried until her fifties and a single mother by choice after adopting a daughter, Gale embodied a woman infused with Suffragette spirit. An active supporter of various women's liberation groups, she employed her power as a writer to explore the frustration of women and the opportunities they lacked.

Lulu Bett's character was a vessel of Gale's mindset within the tale of a 30-year-old 'spinster' being treated as the family slave. But through a story of strong will and a madcap unwitting marriage (proving that preposterous meet-cutes have always been a thing), Lulu rises to independence while telling her family to get stuffed. Despite finding an alternative lover who

doesn't have selective amnesia over the fact he is already married (told you it was nuts), she triumphantly ditches both men, saying, 'Maybe it was just myself I wanted.'

Perhaps demonstrating how such a conclusion was ahead of its time, test audiences for the theatre show weren't ready for such an empowering ending. But while Gale obliged and rewrote it to see Lulu in love, at least it's with someone she actually wants. Pioneering feminist screenplay writer Clara Beranger – noted for 85 screenplays, including 1915's *Anna Karenina* – brought the play to the screen, sustaining Gale's concerns of gender inequality of the time. With Gale being an executive member of the Lucy Stone League, their ethos of encouraging women to keep their name after marriage winks within the humour.

Miss Lulu Bett isn't the only silent romcom busting feminist moves, but with its rubber stamp by the National Film Registry as 'culturally, historically or aesthetically significant', Lulu will forever defend the romcom for leveraging empowered women.

OTHER ROMCOMS TO BINGE:

IT (1927)
Popularizing the idea of the 'it' girl, Clara Bow packed a punch.

DANCE, GIRL, DANCE (1940)
Dorothy Arzner directs Maureen O'Hara and Lucille Ball as two very different dancers contending for integrity and respect.

THE ROMCOM THAT...

PROVED 'WHEN SHE WAS BAD, SHE WAS BETTER'

I'M NO ANGEL

DIRECTOR: Wesley Ruggles
WRITERS: Mae West. 'With suggestions' from Lowell Brentano *(as humorously written in the credits)*
YEAR: 1933

Romcoms have a habit of turning bad girls good after some existential soul-searching that makes them see the error of their ways (here's looking at you, *Trainwreck*), but in Mae West's *I'm No Angel*, which inspired 1930s Hollywood censorship, we see one of the last rewarded displays of a woman's sexual assertiveness for decades.

In this wisecracking romcom infused with West's signature sauce, circus dancer Tira (West) likes her men 'one at a time' but ain't a one-man woman. She even has a selection of records where she sings adoringly of the men of different cities that she can conveniently whack on according to her latest catch's address. As she shimmies from one rich shmuck to the next, she shares gifts from her many admirers with her fellow stage gals, and while the journey from circus to courtroom is fuzzy in its plot, the real spectacle here is Tira's power over men.

Tira may work in the circus, taming vexed lions, but it's the men in this movie that are the ones being whipped. Gyrating on stage, wearing just diamonds and a smile, she makes the eyes of hungry men bulge, before calling them suckers under her breath. It was this show of brazen sexuality (and racial integration) that inspired the prudish censors to start enforcing rules.

Through today's lens, the representation of Black women certainly upholds the racist tropes of mammies, but it was radical for 1930s cinema to see Black and white people get on. And with many Black friends from the vaudeville scene, writing them in such prominent roles was West's way of lifting them up.

West wrote the book on how women could claim their sexuality for themselves, but seeing her name in large font next to 'story, screenplay AND all dialogue' in the opening credits, it's clear that it was her talent for writing she also wanted to flaunt. And from zingers such as 'It's not the men in your life that counts, it's the life in your men' and 'When I'm good I'm very good, when I'm bad I'm better', West forever lives on through her signature quotes.

OTHER ROMCOMS TO BINGE:

SHE DONE HIM WRONG (1933)
Another Mae West banger where she's batting off men like flies.

BELLE OF THE NINETIES (1934)
Honouring her title of being one of the first women to always write the movies she starred in, here West writes herself opposite a slick prizefighter because why the hell not?

MY LITTLE CHICKADEE (1940)
More saucy zingers, courtroom battles and gold digging excellence from her majesty Miss West.

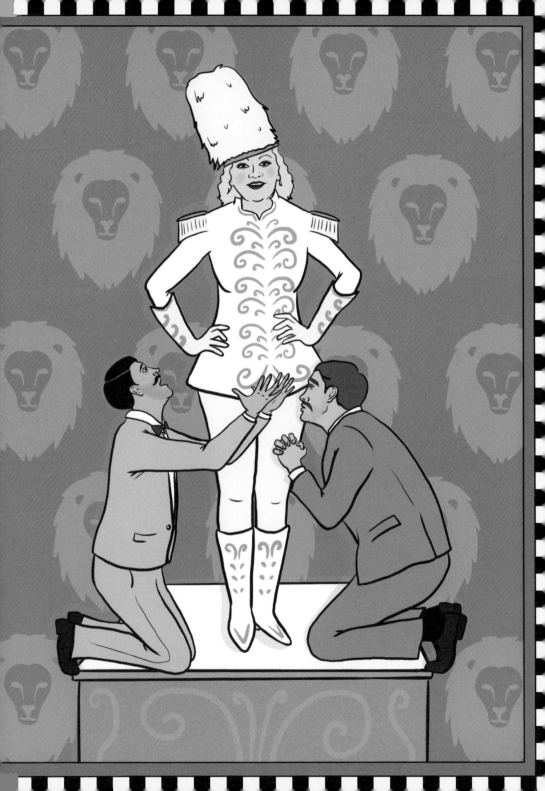

INSPIRED WOMEN TO FIND A SYSTEM OF THEIR OWN

IT HAPPENED ONE NIGHT

DIRECTOR: Frank Capra
WRITERS: Robert Riskin, Samuel Hopkins Adams
YEAR: 1934

In a famous scene in *It Happened One Night*, our screwball protagonists are attempting to hitchhike across America. Peter (a suave, disgruntled newspaper reporter) is trying to school Ellie (a tempestuous young woman fleeing from daddy's yacht) on how to successfully erect her thumb. As cars whizz by, Ellie gets tired and, deciding she's had enough of Peter's unsuccessful showmanship, yanks her skirt up to reveal a shapely shin. As they subsequently hail a ride, Ellie tells a bemused Peter it's her 'system all my own'.

For a film released pre-mainstream feminism, heiress Ellie was a trailblazing representation of someone finding her way using her sexuality and wit – the few powers available to a 1930s woman. Her character (played by megastar Claudette Colbert) bestowed humanity to misunderstood 'poor little rich girls', while suggesting that a woman's freedom to roam provides transformative worldliness – even if she has to jump ship from her privilege and wiggle free from societal cotton wool.

Ellie may have a naive worldview but her Greyhound trip in a post-Depression slump helps her see how the other half live. Eventually, we see her blossom into a self-reflective young woman who knows it's not her fault she's seen as a 'brat'. When she tells Peter (the silky Clark Gable): 'People who are spoiled are accustomed

to having their own way. I never have. I've always been told what to do, and when to do it,' we're reminded of the stifling control forced on so many young girls, while enjoying the spectacle of this one break free.

The premise of a woman (usually clueless, probably clumsy) putting herself out of her comfort zone, and duly coming of age, is a theme we can recognize in so many romantic comedies. That, along with class divides, spontaneous bursts of song and discovering the true meaning of love, all make for a genre that often eats its own tail. But it happened here first in *It Happened One Night*, which – with its five Oscar wins – became the genre's prototype. Only the most successful romantic comedies in its wake have Ellie's essence of a curious spirit, razor-sharp wit and insistence on making their own way in the world.

OTHER ROMCOMS TO BINGE:

I KNOW WHERE I'M GOING! (1945)
Michael Powell and Emeric Pressburger's infamous romance that sees the headstrong Joan find love in a hopeless place.

THE LADY EVE (1941)
Back when screwball comedies made women who talk a lot appealing, Barbara Stanwyck was the con artist with her eye on the prize.

SHE DONE HIM WRONG (1933)
A risqué romcom which saw the tremendous Mae West put her needs before his.

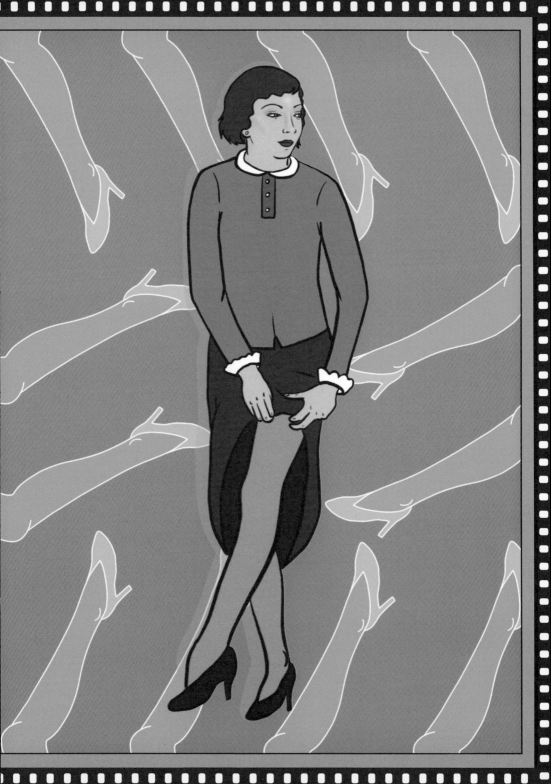

SUPERSEDED MALE DOMINANCE

BRINGING UP BABY

DIRECTOR: Howard Hawks
WRITERS: Dudley Nichols, Hagar Wilde
YEAR: 1938

The term 'screwball' comes from Carl Hubbell – a 1920s New York Giants pitcher with a remarkably unpredictable throw. It soon became shorthand for any cultural phenomenon that took an unexpected turn. It's why *Bringing Up Baby* is the quintessential screwball romcom, as after a slew of Victorianesque screen heroines, Katharine Hepburn's Susan Vance helped female roles take an invigorating twist.

In this bona fide classic, stiff, engaged-to-be-married palaeontologist David (Cary Grant) needs an all-important bone. After learning of a millionaire matron with a spare $1m, he discovers her flutter-brained niece Susan, who's taken quite a shine to him and his brontosaurus. Susan also happens to have a big wild cat called 'Baby', who's hungry for some meat. And if you haven't clocked the innuendo yet, you are but a saint.

In *Bringing Up Baby*, Susan's dandy twist on feminine glamour and energetic masculine bravado both defied and elevated gender norms. In barging her way onto the typically masculine arena of a golf course, seizing David's balls and luring him away from his frigid fiancée, she illuminated a new-age woman who – riffing off some Mae West energy – superseded male dominance while getting herself a man.

There's a fierce romance and captivating audacity in Susan's prowess in capturing an initially reluctant David. When she tells her aunt: 'I know that I'm going to marry him. He doesn't know it, but I am,' we see David try but fail to avoid falling for her goofy, assured charm. As well as the role reversal of a woman confidently on the prowl, Susan constantly subverts male supremacy while fulfilling her own fantasy. In the sports field, driving seat, prison – even the bedroom, where she forces David to wear women's clothes – she strides in and spitballs her way out of every high jinks imaginable.

Bringing Up Baby is a romantic comedy titan, yet it's telling to note it was a flop on release. With the 'failure' being pinned on Hepburn (who was subsequently branded 'box-office poison', while Grant still thrived), it's fair to say people just didn't know how to respond to a woman on the loose.

OTHER ROMCOMS TO BINGE:

SHE DONE HIM WRONG (1933)
When Mae West cooed, 'Why don't you come up sometime and see me?' to Cary Grant, it became her signature line and set a seductive new bar for how women played the field.

TWENTIETH CENTURY (1934)
Or any film starring Carole Lombard, really, but this one, where she plays a divine Hollywood diva, is a screwball prototype.

SHOWED SHE COULD HAVE A CAREER AND A MARRIAGE

HIS GIRL FRIDAY

DIRECTOR: Howard Hawks
WRITERS: Charles Lederer,
Ben Hecht, Charles MacArthur
YEAR: 1940

Sharp style, big hats and more words per minute than an East Coast rapper, Hildy Johnson is among Hollywood's most lauded characters. Played with panache by Rosalind Russell, Hildy crystallized the vision of a woman who was energized by her work. A forthright journalist who knows the power of the press, there's an innate talent to her writing that cannot be suppressed.

Those that recognize the embers of Hildy's passion, but see it at odds with the pressure of settling down, can find catharsis in this classic as a reminder that both are possible. For a representation as such in the stifling 1940s, *His Girl Friday* was a pin-up for career women who also fancied marriage. With the backdrop of a newspaper room during the Second World War, it reflected a time when women gained opportunities in journalism, with many promoted to editors due to the shortage of men.

The source material of *His Girl Friday* had less feminist intent. Inspired by the ambition to remake 1931's *The Front Page* (adapted from the 1928 Broadway show of the same name), the original players were hard-boiled with a cocksure cast of men. But after director Howard Hawks had his secretary read Hildy's lines, he was enlightened to the idea of the part belonging to a woman. This may have been a savvy move, as comedies of remarriage boomed in 1930–1940, but what Hawks couldn't have guessed was that this gender-swap would create one of the most celebrated women-at-work roles still to this day.

It's also a joy to see a woman truly portrayed as an equal, as Hildy's ex-husband editor Walter (Cary Grant) knows she is his ace and finds her all the more appealing (not intimidating) for it. In a plot that sees him talk her off the ledge of suburban wifedom, he tempts her back to the desk with an irresistible story. There are few more satisfying scenes in Hollywood than seeing Hildy ferociously knock out the article while telling her neglected fiancé, 'I'm not a suburban bridge player, I'm a newspaperman!' Spirited back into the world she loves, she naturally remarries the man who knows this will be a three-way relationship: him, her and her typewriter.

OTHER ROMCOMS TO BINGE:

JULIE & JULIA (2009)
For real marriage goals, look to Meryl Streep as celebrity chef Julia Childs whose hubby (Stanley Tucci) is nothing but supportive. A Nora Ephron peach.

MR. MOM (1983)
In a film that may not have aged well, this John Hughes number sees its wife bring home the bacon.

HAD HER WEARING
THE TROUSERS

THE PHILADELPHIA STORY

DIRECTOR: George Cukor
WRITERS: Donald Ogden Stewart,
Philip Barry, Waldo Salt
YEAR: 1940

Off screen and on, literally and proverbially, Katharine Hepburn is someone who wore the trousers. This phrase may reinforce male supremacy, but it was triumphantly reclaimed thanks to Hepburn's penchant for pants. Although her handsome style and blazing persona were clocked way before the arrival of *The Philadelphia Story*, it was this romcom that saw her channel that Goliath energy into a victorious reinvention.

In *The Philadelphia Story* Tracy Lord (Hepburn) is a socialite with three men squabbling for her attention. While due to marry George, pesky ex-husband Dexter returns and soon finds himself contending with the reporter covering her wedding. With three men after her, and that fierce independent charm, there's certainly something about Tracy. But she doesn't want to be worshipped – she wants to be loved, so it's no wonder she chooses the man who makes her feel 'like a human being'.

Written by playwright Philip Barry, with Hepburn in mind, the show lit up the stage before making it to the big screen. With the success of the play, the cinema beckoned, but after her series of box-office 'flops' (including the now revered *Bringing Up Baby*), she knew she'd have to act smart to keep herself in the picture. When her lover Howard Hughes gifted her the film rights, she sold them back to MGM Studios for three times as much. Knowing no one else would hire her, she hired herself and soon she was back up in lights as Tracy Lord. The result? A film that went on to be nominated for six Academy Awards (back when romcoms won awards), and Hepburn going from 'box office poison' to a woman who meant business.

At a time when women in trousers could literally be arrested, slacks-wearing Hepburn was the talk of the town. When previous film studios had tried to confiscate her jeans, she'd just walk onto set in her knickers until they were returned. No such confiscation was required on *The Philadelphia Story* because no one dared argue with Hepburn at the helm. Instead, her gender-blending flair wove into a film that became a beacon for how a woman can be liberated by power, choice and style.

OTHER ROMCOMS TO BINGE:

ADAM'S RIB (1949)
Playing on Hepburn's reputation, the movie poster declares: 'It's the hilarious answer to who wears the pants'.

BRINGING UP BABY (1938, SEE PAGE 22)
Hepburn on the prowl for Cary Grant's bone makes this a sexual-innuendo masterpiece.

HOLIDAY (1938)
More proof that Hepburn and Grant were the Meg and Tom of their time.

GAVE INSIGHT INTO THE INTELLIGENCE OF THE 'BIMBO'

GENTLEMEN PREFER BLONDES

DIRECTOR: Howard Hawks
WRITERS: Charles Lederer, Joseph Fields, Anita Loos
YEAR: 1953

If there's any doubt to the pretext to *Gentlemen Prefer Blondes*, the opening number sung by Marilyn Monroe and Jane Russell, waxes some advice: 'Find a gentleman who is shy or bold, or short or tall, or young or old, as long as the guy's a millionaire!' Gold diggers? Our blonde Lorelei is more into diamonds, but she'll take it. But if you thought our bombshell double act were bimbos (and not in the recently reclaimed Gen Z sense), they've got you fooled too.

Within a carousel of lipsticked one-liners and ravishing outfits, best friends Lorelei and Dorothy are sailing to the 'Isle de Paris', where Lorelei is to marry a millionaire dork. While she's busy mining the diamonds of alternative suitors (because every woman needs an insurance policy), brunette Dorothy is more interested in being serenaded by the all-male Olympic team. As they bat their eyelashes at the men, while secretly rolling their eyes at each other, these partners in crime pout their way to financial stability. And why not? In a post-Second World War environment where women were shooed back into the kitchen – and away from lucrative careers – was it wrong to use the limited power that society afforded them to secure a comfortable life?

The source material of Anita Loos' 1926 best-selling satirical novel lampoons the point that stupidity is performed by someone smart enough to manipulate men. And while some may pity the fools who fall for their trap, just remember the bimbo rules; only use men who have nothing to lose.

But what of love? Dorothy asks on our behalf. 'If a girl spends time worrying about the money she doesn't have, how will she have any time for love?' is Lorelei's witty defence that sees her intellect start to leak, and in a nod to the fragility of men who find women with brains a threat, she later says 'I can be smart when it's important, but most men don't like it.'

The romances Dorothy and Lorelei flirt with are nothing in comparison to the chemistry between our girls, and as they harmonize their way through the conclusion that 'men are the same everywhere', they marry in a double wedding, while giving a wink to each other and us.

OTHER ROMCOMS TO BINGE:

HOW TO MARRY A MILLIONAIRE (1953)
Marilyn Monroe, Lauren Bacall and Betty Grable provide the manual.

BARBIE (2023, SEE PAGE 214)
Proving the Barbie doll was always more than just a pretty face.

GOLD DIGGERS OF 1933 (1933)
Joan Blondell and her showgirl pals put on a song and dance about digging for Depression-era gold.

LIBERATED THE SEXUAL FREEDOM OF 1950S WOMEN

PILLOW TALK

DIRECTOR: Michael Gordon
WRITERS: Stanley Shapiro, Maurice Richlin, Russell Rouse
YEAR: 1959

Once upon a time, Hollywood liked to pretend it didn't know where babies came from. Using morality measure the Hays Code between 1934 and the mid-1960s, 'lustful kissing, scenes of passion, nudity and discussions of sexual perversity' were outlawed in a film, in case they lowered the 'moral standards of those who see it'. While film-makers got creative with suggestive tact, a woman's sexual expression on film was far from free.

As the rules relaxed (when the Supreme Court decided films were protected by freedom of speech), up popped *Pillow Talk*. Pinging open with a shot of Doris Day's shapely leg, this technicolour gobstopper kicked the 1950s housewife off a cliff. In the first of a hat-trick of films that starred Rock Hudson and Day, *Pillow Talk* was the flint that set their on-screen affair alight and broke our blonde away from the wholesome girl-next-door.

As a successful interior decorator, Jan earns enough to live alone and have a hilarious – if drunk – housekeeper. As she shimmies from scene to scene in her jaw-dropping outfits (including the biggest muffs ever), we see her turn down advances from the kind of men who casually buy her cars. At a time when a woman's wealth lent towards her marrying well, here Jan was making her own mint. That's not to say she won't give guys a whirl, but if a kiss doesn't make her feel like she's 'hit the moon', she goes on her merry way.

Jan's indifference to marriage is also a boon, and while previous films bent over backwards to ignore premarital sex, Jan's up for a dirty weekend with a man she's just met. That trip is with Brad (Hudson) – the cad serenading women on her pesky shared crosswire phone line, but while she's yet to realize that punk is the same guy she's now dating, she unwittingly inspires him to want to grow up.

With an Oscar nomination for Best Actress, and *Pillow Talk* going on to be one of the highest-grossing films of the year, critics and audiences were ready for a new Day. And as she peeled off the skin of her former saintly self, she contributed to a fresh archetype of a woman who had 'no bedroom problems'.

OTHER ROMCOMS TO BINGE:

SOME LIKE IT HOT (1959)
As the Hays Code became old hat, Tony Curtis and Jack Lemmon got busy with cross-dressing – 1959 was a good year for shaking up Hollywood.

SEND ME NO FLOWERS (1964)
Building on that assertiveness we began to see in Day's characters, again she gives as good as she gets against Rock.

LOVER COME BACK (1961)
More proof that the Rock/Day chemistry wasn't a fluke.

STUCK IT TO 'THE MAN'

THE APARTMENT

DIRECTOR: Billy Wilder
WRITERS: Billy Wilder, I.A.L. Diamond
YEAR: 1960

Paying $84 a month for rent when your pay is $94.70? Blame it on The Man. Hit a glass ceiling working as an elevator attendant? That'll be The Man. These are the scenarios of *The Apartment's* Fran (Shirley MacLaine) and C.C. Baxter (Jack Lemmon) who are tangled in a system that is set to keep them down; yet when Fran finds her ally in Baxter and Baxter sacrifices his privileges, we're given licence to dream about telling patriarchal power where to go and see a true romcom hero who deserves to get the girl.

Aptly set within the 'Consolidated Life' insurance company, employee Baxter rents an apartment that he rarely gets to use. His nebbish persona is constantly taken advantage of by various superiors, who use his home as an extramarital den. As a reward for being endlessly out in the cold while his bosses cheat on their wives, he's either bribed with a promotion or blackmailed with the sack. As Baxter's unearned promotions are based on him keeping schtum, it reflects the cronyism that makes Boys' Clubs thrive.

The Apartment is a sublime example of how the deft hand of romcom can grapple with big topics with Fairy-soft hands, and in cutting through the grease of society's ills, we see how capitalist corporations are engineered by a small bunch of conniving men. But none are slimier than Mr Sheldrake, whose affair with elevator girl Fran leads to an attempt on her own life. Perhaps a bit dramatic for the average romcom, but the mood is lifted when Baxter uses a tennis racket to strain her spaghetti. Of course, this is because Baxter hearts Fran, who's realized he's been complicit in a system that undermines women and schmucks like him. So he takes the advice of his neighbour, who's a doctor, and decides to be a 'mensch' – meaning human and not yet another patriarchal prat.

After some pirouetting twists leading to a symbolic New Year's Eve, Fran and Baxter independently ditch Sheldrake, so it's him who's out in the cold. In unwittingly discovering they've both stuck it to the proverbial 'Man', their acts of liberation find them in love and with a new pack of cards to 'shut up and deal'.

OTHER ROMCOMS TO BINGE:

OUTSOURCED (2006)
An American call-centre manager gets a wake-up call on corporate life. Meeting the beautiful Asha on his business trip to India certainly helps.

IRMA LA DOUCE (1963)
Using the premise of a policeman in love with a sex worker, Wilder, MacLaine and Lemmon reunite for morality mayhem.

PIONEERED THE BACHELORETTE PAD

BREAKFAST AT TIFFANY'S

DIRECTOR: Blake Edwards
WRITERS: Truman Capote, George Axelrod
YEAR: 1961

Some cultural icons transcend their source material, as perfectly demonstrated by Audrey Hepburn's Miss Holly Golightly. With that little black dress, huge sunglasses and the sleeping mask over those I've-not-been-to-bed eyes, Holly is the epitome of aristocratic chic, whether you've seen *Breakfast at Tiffany's* or not. This vision has outshone the depth of the film, which radically presented a woman with a room of her own. And at a time when a woman's cinematic uniform was an apron and a grin, Holly contributed to the movement that kicked the wholesome housewife to the curb.

In her own New York apartment bought by serenading, naive, thirsty men, go-hard Golightly has been compared to *The Great Gatsby* in drag. She drinks, throws wild parties and is a disinterested cook, muttering, 'I've taken care of myself a long time' to those who try to intervene. Considering a woman's historical 'role' had long been that of a housewife, it's telling when the agent who failed to tame her brands her apartment a 'dump'. But an eccentric minimalist pad big enough to swing her ginger cat in is, by today's standards, a dream that no 20-something can afford.

The relaxation of the Hays Code (see page 31) worked in favour of the screen adaptation of Truman Capote's far racier novella. Holly's fancy men and nightgowns presented a woman free to relish her femininity for herself and for others. With no husband, kids or parents, she can use her home as she pleases – a luxury she can appreciate after escaping the life of a child bride.

The iconography of Golightly suggests a truly independent woman, so you'll be forgiven for forgetting that the film ends with her being saved by a man. While this is at odds with the more ambiguous and feminist reading of the book, at least he's her equal and also in the business of socializing the rich and horny.

The feminism might be divisive, but the racism ain't, as Mickey Rooney's caricature of Mr Yunioshi is the film's jarring stain. So, again, we're here making necessary pointers to the past that add context to historical racism that pop culture helped engineer.

OTHER ROMCOMS TO BINGE:

THE WEDDING PLANNER (2001)
The film that tried to make us feel sorry for Jennifer Lopez's solo living, when actually it just made her look like a boss.

PILLOW TALK (1959, SEE PAGE 30)
More solo-living luxury from Doris Day's apartment (back when romcoms didn't treat women living alone as an excuse to present a fleapit).

THE HOLIDAY (2006, SEE PAGE 128)
Two exceptionally beautiful homes, owned by independent women, for the price of one.

CHALLENGED THE IDEA OF THE 'OLDER WOMAN'

HAROLD AND MAUDE

DIRECTOR: Hal Ashby
WRITER: Colin Higgins
YEAR: 1971

As depictions of older women and their love lives fail to meaningfully manifest, we'll have to settle on looking back to the outliers that tried to pave a way. They don't get more unconventional than this 1971 oddball which sees a morbid 19-year-old boy fall for a woman nearing 80. As they meet within their shared pastime of gatecrashing funerals, they build a surprisingly beautiful relationship that blossoms into love.

And what's not to love about the eccentric Maude, what with her stories of activism and enthusiasm for life? Through the outlook of our heroine, we all learn about living and the enlightenment that is unlocked when we appreciate what makes us unique. As Harold's mother tries to marry him off, and his uncle tries to draft him into the army, Maude provides an alternative view of what masculinity can be: to reject such labels entirely and – among her many other life affirmations – 'try something new each day. After all, we're given life to find it out. It doesn't last forever'.

This is where Maude gets somewhat divisive, as she loves life enough to know when her own should cease. But whatever your take is on her deciding to end her own life at 80 ('because it's a nice round number'), she makes it hard for anyone to argue with her ultimate act of independence. Maude is what we could call an original 'strong female character', before the phrase became tarnished by visions of women who could hold a gun and their beer. As for the topic of cinematic clichés that beckon debate, Maude could be misdiagnosed as a manic pixie dream girl with more grey hair than most. On the contrary, her life of 'picket lines and rallies' sees her character motivated by more than simply giving Harold a reason to live.

It's an omission by Western standards not to hail our elders, not to mention overlook the fact that they still get the horn. Yet, Maude is spirited, self-possessed and bent on breaking down boundaries, and – in an unfetishized slant on an octogenarian's sex life – she is still able to make young men blow bubbles in a post-coital glow.

OTHER ROMCOMS TO BINGE:

GOOD LUCK TO YOU, LEO GRANDE (2022, SEE PAGE 208)
A breakthrough sexual comedy that sees a 60-year-old woman find her sexual awakening.

FEAR EATS THE SOUL (1974)
A searing oddball older romance which sees love vs racism.

LE WEEK-END (2013)
A little saucy, somewhat sophisticated, but ultimately touching romcom about a long-term marriage.

HIGHLIGHTED A BROKEN WELFARE SYSTEM

CLAUDINE

DIRECTOR: John Berry
WRITERS: Tina Pine, Lester Pine
YEAR: 1974

In 1970s America, the welfare system was a joke. Single mothers who worked outside the home couldn't claim any benefits; meanwhile, most jobs available to young women of colour didn't pay minimum wage. It was a lose-lose situation that, although it sounds bleak, still managed to create a beaming portrait of resilience under the umbrella of a social-realist romcom.

In a genre that frequently explores the class divide, here was a self-proclaimed 'heart and soul comedy' that placed its lovers in the same working-class boat. Set in 1970s Harlem, we meet Claudine (Diahann Carroll) after she has seen each of her six kids off for their day. Cut to the glistening biceps of garbage collector Roop (James Earl Jones), whom she agrees to date, if only to get that sexual 'vitamin F' fix. As they court over takeaway chicken in his mouse-infested flat, a squabble lets us know they're aware of the stereotype they present. She may be 'popping out those babies for the taxpayer to take care of', while he's 'just another Black stud' who doesn't see his kids. Yet, after cheering them on for an affectionate 90 minutes, *Claudine* adds dynamics to these racist associations.

The development of their affair presents a lectern for the film's message. How are people on welfare supposed to live, let alone love, when the system is broken? After another sleepover that sees them sneak around like kids (they're frequently in a post-coital glow), she jokes that she's married to the welfare man who has her in a bind: 'If I can't feed my kids, it's child neglect. If I go out and get myself a little job on the side, and don't tell him, then I'm cheating. If I stay at home, then I'm lazy.' And when Claudine's social worker pops round for a snoop, she has to hide Roop in the toilet, in case they suspect he's providing funds.

Helmed by Third World Cinema Corporation, *Claudine* met the studio's aim to humanize people of colour on screen. And with a score specifically written by Curtis Mayfield and performed by Gladys Knight & the Pips, it provided music to the ears of anyone tired of one-note romcoms that had kept films like *Claudine* out.

OTHER ROMCOMS TO BINGE:

ALI & AVA (2021)
More love in a hopeless place – this time on the housing estates of Bradford. British romantic dramedy at its blistering best.

I LIKE IT LIKE THAT (1994)
A love letter to New York that finds hilarity and drama in juggling motherhood and love.

JULIA (1968-71)
Diahann Carroll shines as a single mum in the first TV series to star a Black woman as something more than a maid.

OUTED SEXUAL
DOUBLE STANDARDS

SHE'S GOTTA HAVE IT

DIRECTOR: Spike Lee
WRITER: Spike Lee
YEAR: 1986

The only reason Nola Darling is consenting to this movie is because she wants 'to clear her name and if, in the end, it helps some other people out, well, then, that's fine, too'. This is how Spike Lee's sexual-politics comedy introduces us to our heroine, while immediately presenting a sisterhood to women also branded as 'freaks'. But what's really so freakish about enjoying multiple sexual partners? Haven't men enjoyed this liberty for years?

These double standards were arrestingly explored in this 1986 classic. Igniting Lee's confronting oeuvre, his first feature was dedicated to hailing a Black woman's sexuality while reflecting the hypocrisy, sexism and racism that they often receive. Nola was a radical protagonist within a shallow pool of depictions of polyamorous women, let alone Black women with sexual autonomy. With her three men and one hopeful woman, she casually gets her kicks with those who crave her time. Through confessional anecdotes to us from each character, we hear the many points of view of those in Nola's orbit.

What's comically rich is that people around her try to diagnose her behaviour as a defect from birth. From assuming she had a bad relationship with her father, to the fact she 'crawled backwards before she could walk',

we see the sweeping judgements made about women who like carefree sex. To humour us all, Nola visits a therapist who determines that she's just a healthy human being. Not that it satisfies one of her fuck buddies, who exclaims, 'A female doctor? What does she know?!'

The one thing the three men share is their frustration with not being able to pin Nola down – and this is reflective of a world that tries to cage a Black woman's sex. At its most menacing, this leaks into a divisive scene that sees Nola's 'near rape' (as she coins it) from the man most emasculated by her refusal to commit. It interrupts an otherwise profound film and has caused a wiser Spike Lee to admit regret. At last, with relief, Nola's character tells him where to go and concludes with, 'My body, my mind. Who was gonna own it? Them or me? I am not a one-man woman.'

OTHER ROMCOMS TO BINGE:

SHE'S GOTTA HAVE IT (2017-19)
An older and wiser Spike Lee works on his 'immature' dealings with consent in a new Nola Darling for the Netflix generation.

THINK LIKE A MAN (2012)
This modern romance caper confronts stuffy gendered roles.

CRAZY, STUPID, LOVE (2011)
A grown-up romcom with a side-eye view on dating standards.

40

BATTLED CAREER VS MOTHERHOOD

BABY BOOM

DIRECTOR: Charles Shyer
WRITERS: Charles Shyer, Nancy Meyers
YEAR: 1987

As births boomed in the 1980s, so did movies about the catastrophe of children. But as ticklish as *Three Men and a Baby* and *Honey, I Shrunk the Kids* were, *Baby Boom* dropped the bomb on how motherhood vs career was the new gender war.

This successful 1980s smash, written by Nancy Meyers and her husband after the birth of their daughter, follows J.C. (Diane Keaton) who inherits a baby from a long-lost relative. Thing is, J.C. is about as maternal as an abortion clinic and has worked too hard in her nine-to-five to risk her six-figure salary. When her boss sizes her up for a promotion, but is worried she might want kids and a husband, she goes to great lengths to insist, 'I don't want it all.'

'Having it all' meant not having to choose between parenthood and career, as rising feminism championed the idea of achieving both. But what *Baby Boom* hammers home with a slapstick thwack is that even though '53 per cent of the American workforce is female', those at the top are still men, who expect women to work 80 hours a week.

Anyone who knows the mega cost of childcare and the toil of raising a baby knows that working more than you sleep is impossible – especially as a single parent, as J.C. finds herself after being dumped.

This is where *Baby Boom* gets progressive. J.C. doesn't sacrifice her entrepreneurial streak and when she relocates to Vermont (to 'bake apple pies and get into quilts'), she uses the romanticism she applied to her rash country move to sell overpriced gourmet baby food to yuppies. When her old bosses try to buy her now multi-million-dollar business, she assesses the life she's made with her daughter and new lover (Sam Shepard), and sees she's rewired the system to balance work, love and motherhood in her own version of having it all.

In a world where career opportunities still dwindle after parenthood, *Baby Boom* dared to dream. In one of the many sermons that delivers truth to the bedlam of parenthood vs career, J.C. tells the board 'I don't wanna make sacrifices. The bottom line is nobody should have to.'

OTHER ROMCOMS TO BINGE:

BABY DONE (2020)
When an unexpected baby upends her adventurous streak, Rose Matafeo sets herself a bucket list, proving how pesky pregnancy is.

LIFE AS WE KNOW IT (2010)
Only a romcom could bypass the tragedy of an orphan to create an elaborate meet-cute.

PARALLEL MOTHERS (2021)
Two women, two different circumstances, one stylish observation of the nature vs nurture of motherhood from Pedro Almodóvar.

EMBRACED HER CAREER
AS HER FIRST LOVE

BROADCAST NEWS

DIRECTOR: James L. Brooks
WRITER: James L. Brooks
YEAR: 1987

The year is 1983 and director James L. Brooks is sensing something in the air. 'Feminism was happening,' he tells *The Ringer* journalist Haley Mlotek. 'There had to be a female heroine around. I went looking for her.' Four years on, and after extensively hanging out with female broadcast journalists, Holly Hunter was cast as a woman who put her career first.

Just 5ft 2in tall but with giant woman energy, Jane is our heroine who bleeds newspaper ink. Clinging to ethical reporting within the dawn of celebrity news, Jane and her colleague Aaron are 'not there "to stage the news".' But as the industry starts to put looks above brains, in steps reporter Tom, who's just a pretty face. And so we have our love triangle where Jane's ethics are tested, as she has to decide if she can elope with Mr Fake News.

The fast pace of the newsroom is breathlessly captured but it's Jane and her female colleagues making it work. Feeding lines to male reporters, aiming the camera or making breakneck edits with 52 seconds to go, women are the chefs behind each meaty bit of news. Within these scenes, where everything is invisible until that deadline is met, Jane is truly alive and in those quieter moments, when adrenaline ebbs, her diarized sobs help her loosen a valve. It's a nod to hard-working women who recognize that with

high pressure comes the need for a release. Jane is facetiously asked if it's nice being the smartest person in the room, and she responds, 'No, it's awful,' with sincere exasperation.

Jane's true love is a reciprocal one with her career. When she walks away from both men, it's because one would mean settling and the other would go against her integrity – and probably for the best when, seven years on, she's talking wistfully about a new man who could be The One. It's glorious to see a romcom treat work ethic with respect (and consistent promotions), where others see career women as something of a threat. Instead, it's the thing that makes Jane so mesmerizing, because isn't everyone most beautiful when doing what they love?

OTHER ROMCOMS TO BINGE:

MORNING GLORY (2010)
More TV broadcast mayhem with Rachel McAdams in the producer seat. Speaking into the ear of Harrison Ford has never looked like such hard work.

RAISING ARIZONA (1987)
Here Holly Hunter's character's first love is becoming a mother, which she does with equally manic (and illegal) persistence.

LATE NIGHT (2019)
A workplace comedy brought up to date with the politics of glass ceilings when you're a woman of colour. Mindy Kaling shines.

44

LIBERATED THE 'WALK OF SHAME'

MOONSTRUCK

DIRECTOR: Norman Jewison
WRITER: John Patrick Shanley
YEAR: 1987

The dictionary definition of the 'walk of shame' is: 'The return trip home the morning after an unplanned sexual encounter, usually a one-night stand, wearing clothing from the previous evening.' Although none of that sentence is gendered, it has been disproportionately applied to women, in yet another example of how their sexual encounters have forever been judged.

In 2017 'The Maga[luf] Walk of Shame' Facebook page made headlines after posting images of women walking back to their hotel. There's even a film of the same name that, over a hateful 95 minutes, sees Elizabeth Banks constantly mistaken for a sex worker thanks to last night's outfit seeing the light of day. But, sigh, let's not let a little thing like sexism distract us from the big heart of *Moonstruck* because in this complex, passionate movie that won Cher an Oscar there's no time wasted on belittling its women.

In probably the least judgemental film about women and people's bed-traversing antics, *Moonstruck* sees 37-year-old widow Loretta (Cher) – an Italian-American Brooklynite who's done with love – about to sell herself short by marrying man-child Johnny (Danny Aiello), who needs a surrogate mum. But when Johnny's neurotic younger brother Ronny (Nicolas Cage) explodes onto the scene, their chemistry is bombastic as they find themselves intertwined. After succumbing to a date at the opera, a tuxedoed Ronny rages with Shakespearian passion: 'We are here to ruin ourselves and to break our hearts and love the wrong people and DIE!' There was only one thing Loretta could do after he follows it up with, 'Now get in my bed!'

As Loretta walks home in last night's glow-up – which, btw, is a chef's kiss self-transformation – it is in this new dawn that she is finally free. Free from her self-imposed omens, free from self-restraint and – in spite of her suppressed romanticism – free from the idea that her one shot at love was run over by a bus (RIP). As the bedazzling red shoes she bought for the occasion ferry her home, she may as well not need them, as she looks set to float. Despite leaving the bed of her fiancé's brother to come home, it's not shame she feels, but 'I love him awful' love.

OTHER ROMCOMS TO BINGE:

BREAKFAST AT TIFFANY'S (1961, SEE PAGE 34)
Who doesn't stop to gaze at the Tiffany's shop window while walking home at 5 a.m.?

BREAD AND TULIPS (2000)
Where it was more a hitchhike home than a walk of shame.

HOW TO BE SINGLE (2016, SEE PAGE 168)
Where Rebel Wilson's way of waking up at other people's houses is an art.

GAVE GASLIGHTING ITS DEADLY REVENGE

HEATHERS

DIRECTOR: Michael Lehmann
WRITER: Daniel Waters
YEAR: 1988

For anyone unclear of what gaslighting is, *Heathers* provides a retro example of how deadly it can be. In this barbed hybrid romance that crushed high school, coming of age and black comedy into one, the teenage Winona Ryder (Veronica) provides dark-hearted revenge for anyone who has fallen for that trick.

Observing high-school cliques with a Machiavellian squint, the Heathers are the cool-girl cohort who reign. Veronica is in the club but she's dying to get out and, when she spots the James Dean lookalike 'J.D.' (Christian Slater), she thinks she may have found her escape. J.D. is an alluring mix and Veronica is wooed by his cynicism on conformity. But when she gets sucked into his deadly game of killing off the douchebags, he's soon making her feel like *she's* the guilty one.

J.D. represents a manipulative pressure we've seen men employ for years to belittle women. With gaslighting meaning 'a form of emotional abuse that causes a victim to question themselves', J.D. is here hot-handedly holding the torch. After wanting to get her own back on the boys that assaulted her, Veronica agrees to J.D.'s game of luring them into the woods. But when the gun she's given shoots bullets and not blanks, J.D. tells her, 'You believed it because you wanted to believe it! Your true feelings were too gross and icky for you to face.'

After more murders staged as suicides, Veronica's eventual fury makes a compelling watch. Pulling the rug from a succession of agreeable John Hughes heroines (*Sixteen Candles, The Breakfast Club* and *Pretty in Pink*), Veronica raged against the machine by refusing to tolerate toxic fuck-boy behaviour. In an infectious script, she finishes on an explosive high, telling J.D., 'You know what I want, babe? Cool guys like you out of my life.'

Of course, gaslighting isn't a gendered weapon, but its inception did come from a male character. After the 1938 play *Gaslight* inspired three film adaptations, the concept of the protagonist mentally abusing his wife evolved into a verb. As its now-frequent use is often pithy and misplaced, allow these films to demonstrate – and thus intercept – how psychologically damaging the gaslighting process can be.

OTHER ROMCOMS TO BINGE:

GASLIGHT (1944)
Arguably the most superior of the play's three remakes, with Ingrid Bergman as the victim of the mind games.

THE STEPFORD WIVES (1975)
Took gaslighting to the extreme.

OVERBOARD (2018)
Revenge for the 1987 original, Anna Faris does a gender-swap solid and provides a reality check to a man above his station.

TAUGHT WOMEN TO RECOGNIZE THEIR WORTH

MYSTIC PIZZA

DIRECTOR: Donald Petrie
WRITERS: Amy Holden Jones, Perry Howze, Randy Howze
YEAR: 1988

A good base, decent cheese ratio and a secret ingredient you can't quite identify make for the most fulfilling of romcoms. Here in the deep cut of *Mystic Pizza*, which launched the careers of Julia Roberts, Lili Taylor and Annabeth Gish, it's served with a hearty helping of feminist sauce.

Within the layers, we witness three significant love lessons of sisters Kat and Daisy, and their friend Jojo. As they enter womanhood, they earn their keep in a humble restaurant called Mystic Pizza run by mother figure Leona, who's taking her secret recipe to retirement. Within each woman lies a slice of familiarity to anyone who knows what it's like to edge into an archetype – be it 'good girl' Kat, 'wild child' Daisy or hybrid of the two Jojo, who's fresh on the boat of 1980s feminism and ready to fight the system.

When Daisy realizes preppy boyfriend Charles is using her as an act of rebellion against his snooty parents, she's wise enough to challenge being treated as poverty porn. As for Jojo, her no sex-before-marriage fiancé Bill is desperate to wed, but she'd rather have fun with his 'thick strong wrists' first. When he paints 'nympho' on the side of his boat, she screams, 'I don't have to marry an asshole. It's the 80s,' later negotiating her terms and conditions of their eventual marriage. Then there's Yale-bound Kat who has the quandary of accepting the babysitting 'wages' from the increasingly creepy married man she's fallen for. While the money will fund her entry to college, she decides she can't be bought and, with a little female solidarity, we know she'll make it on her own.

Within these relationships we see women finally knowing their worth. Despite a world of living up to expectations – from their conservative first-generation Portuguese family to the rules of God-fearing wedlock and even the critique of an old white male food critic – each of these women comes of age with an inspirational spirit. They may have spent a lifetime guessing what that secret pizza ingredient is, but seeing them standing side by side while looking up to the stars, we get the impression they already know it.

OTHER ROMCOMS TO BINGE:

PRACTICAL MAGIC (1998)
Less pizza, more magic – but just as big a slice of female solidarity.

STEEL MAGNOLIAS (1989)
Small town, big hair, a mad wedding and a bunch of incredible women: Julia Roberts, Dolly Parton, Sally Field and Shirley MacLaine.

ALICE DOESN'T LIVE HERE ANYMORE (1974)
As close to a romcom as Martin Scorsese gets, here we see Alice (Ellen Burstyn) learn to put herself first, with a little help from her friends.

PROVED YOU CAN MAKE YOUR OWN OPPORTUNITIES

WORKING GIRL

DIRECTOR: Mike Nichols
WRITER: Kevin Wade
YEAR: 1988

On the Staten Island Ferry in 1985, screenwriter Kevin Wade noted the sneakers that smart office-bound women wore on a commute. It's an observation that led to this acclaimed romcom that highlighted how women have had to create their own opportunities to land leadership roles.

In a rousing opening scene, women with ambitions as big as their hair sail on the ferry towards Wall Street. They fill the boat, but they're missing from the boardrooms, as we soon see the disparity between where men and women sit in corporate 1980s America.

Tess (Melanie Griffith) studies by night, works as an assistant by day and has accepted the fact she'll have to work harder to get ahead. She frequently points out how people don't want to hear from 'just some secretary', despite her smart ideas and further education. With a huge perm and shoulder pads to overcompensate how small the world makes her feel, Tess craves an employer who won't feel her up in the back of a limo. Thankfully, she finds herself assisting the powerful Katharine Parker (Sigourney Weaver), but when Katharine steals Tess's business idea, revenge is sought via a bout of identity theft.

In a familiar romcom premise, Tess fakes Katharine's role while she's off with a broken leg. But before we accuse her of doing a *Single White Female*, let's relish her growing confidence when she sees she can walk the walk. After years of being undermined by male colleagues, Tess created an opportunity no one was willing to provide. After cajoling back her idea and delivering it as her own, she lands a promotion and wins Katharine's ex (Harrison Ford).

Indeed, it's a killjoy to see women at war and, interestingly, the first drafts of Katharine were written for a man – instead, we see that it's one in, one out for women up top.

To cleanse this dated palate, we end on some solidarity, in another interesting gender swap: Tess's new assistant, Alice, had originally been written for a 'Ben'. In answer to her question on what is expected of her, Tess smiles and says, 'I don't expect you to fetch me coffee unless you're getting some for yourself.'

OTHER ROMCOMS TO BINGE:

BABY BOOM (1987, SEE PAGE 42)
Of course the equation gets more tricky when there's a baby involved, but this is the romcom that saw a mother thrive.

MAID IN MANHATTAN (2002, SEE PAGE 112)
With a little push from her friends, this Cinderella made it to the ball and the manager's office.

SET IT UP (2018, SEE PAGE 182)
Where the biggest opportunity she made for herself was actually to quit.

CHANGED THE WAY WE TALKED ABOUT ORGASMS

WHEN HARRY MET SALLY

DIRECTOR: Rob Reiner
WRITER: Nora Ephron
YEAR: 1989

In this bona fide jewel in the romcom crown, the age-old question of whether men and women can ever really be friends is so deliciously chewy that it gets stuck in your teeth. But it's *that* fake-orgasm scene that got people talking and, to this day, still proudly keeps the lights on at Katz's deli in New York where people come again and again (ahem) to 'have what she's having'.

It was Meg Ryan herself who suggested her fake orgasm wasn't just discussed over a mouthful of meticulously ordered food, but performed. Beyond creating one of the most memorable moments in film – period – it served to rouse her character's sexual agency. Before this orgasmic moment, Sally is portrayed as a bit of a prude. Yet, after spanking the table and stunning the restaurant into silence with her pornographic yells, we become aware that we're watching someone who knows the difference between good and bad sex.

And so a conversation on whether women fake orgasms was unleashed, rudely popping the bubble of men, like Harry, who thought they could take women 'to a place that wasn't human'.

Sally took one for the team on behalf of all those who have felt the need to fake a climax and awkwardly smile away the question of 'Did you ...?' She has also subverted the idea that Harry knows exactly what an orgasm looks and sounds like – and, considering he told his buddy that he makes women 'meow', he probably took his reference points from typically operatic pornography. As Sally finishes her performance, Harry – for the first time in the film – is finally speechless. At last, he realizes that, actually, he might not know everything about women.

The scene offers a unifying moment to women who have endured the facade of sexual gratification for various reasons. Of course, the act of faking an orgasm isn't exactly feminist, and Sally's provocative showcase raises a lot of important questions: why should someone put the egotistical gratification of a man above their own authentic climax? And why is an orgasm seen as the apex of a sexual encounter, when there's plenty of satisfaction to be had without one? These are valid debates and constructive conversations – ones that, thanks to Sally's rude awakening – were more acceptable to have.

OTHER ROMCOMS TO BINGE:

THE TO DO LIST (2013, SEE PAGE 154)
The audacious teen flick that saw Aubrey Plaza do her homework to find her own sexual apex.

THE SESSIONS (2012)
This sweet and candid comedy explores sex and desire when living with a disability.

EMBODIED THE NEW AGE OF 1980S FEMINIST POWER

PRETTY WOMAN

DIRECTOR: Garry Marshall
WRITER: J.F. Lawton
YEAR: 1990

Pretty Woman is the feminist punchbag of the romcom genre. With the same awe that came with discovering Julia Roberts, many were appalled at this golden girl for playing Vivian Ward – a sex worker who struck gold with billionaire Edward Lewis.

For something that never claimed to be a documentary, *Pretty Woman* gets a lot of stick for glamourizing sex work, which says more about a lack of adequate representations if looking to romcoms to provide truth. It's also charged with being a carnival of capitalism, but it was the 1980s and that was the vibe.

Vivian provides a caricature of what 1980s feminism gave women the power to be. With misogyny at large and the term 'sex sells' as marketing 101, some women – with hyper-sexuality and career opportunities on the rise – could challenge the patriarchy by embracing power through sex appeal and money through work. When Vivian combines the two, she enters the rat race to find it's full of men who also screw people for money. The difference? She knows where to draw the line.

When Edward makes judgements or takes her for granted, Vivian is firm in her mantra: 'I say who! I say how much! I run my life!' It presents her masterclass in consent, boundaries and safe sex (a 'buffet of safety' in

fact) – coming from a woman in a profession where it matters most.

The more retro *Pretty Woman* gets, the more this idea transcends. Anyone suggesting Vivian as a 1980s feminist icon in the 1990s would have had to shout over the elated noise of Girl Power TM, and our preoccupation with binaries in the 2000s didn't leave much room for fluid thought. So, here's to the radicalism of nuance and the benefit of hindsight. Vivian was never a woman that needed anyone's pity or deserved judgement, and looking back at how capitalism bred toxic masculinity, we're more likely to ridicule Edward, who buys champagne but doesn't drink it.

This Cinderella story ends with a feminist twist when it's *her* who saves *him* by pulling his cold body from a world of deceit. As he apologizes for everything by climbing up her stairs, he asks, 'What happened after he climbed up the tower and rescued her?' As she meets him halfway (she's all about equality), she replies, 'She rescues him right back.'

OTHER ROMCOMS TO BINGE:

MAID IN MANHATTAN (2002, SEE PAGE 112)
Another misunderstood Cinderella story – he may have been rich, but Marisa never needed saving. And like our Viv, didn't she deserve it?

AMERICAN GIGOLO (1980)
Richard Gere as a sex worker. Did he get any backlash? Did he fuck. Funny what a gender reversal says about bias.

GAVE BLACK WOMEN MONEY, POWER, SEX AND LOVE

BOOMERANG

DIRECTOR: Reginald Hudlin
WRITERS: Barry W. Blaustein, David Sheffield, Eddie Murphy
YEAR: 1992

Before the 1990s, roles for Black women in mainstream Hollywood were slim. As for affording them with any sexual independence, *She's Gotta Have It* was still an anomaly. But *Boomerang* was the film that raised the bar and, using its weight as the first studio all-Black-cast romcom, gave its Black women what they'd long been denied: money, power, sex and love.

It's all the more accentuated within a plot of reversed gender clichés. Marcus (Eddie Murphy) is a talented marketing exec who is as good at bedding women as he is at his job, but his match is met when he encounters the mighty Jacqueline (Robin Givens), who becomes his boss and then lover when their companies merge. Suddenly, it's Marcus who's being objectified and having to sleep his way to the top, and eventually left heartbroken when he realizes he's been used as a toy.

Boomerang didn't just rally a gauntlet of fine Black women actors, it also summoned cultural goddesses and let them strut along stages of corporate wealth. From the prowess of singer Eartha Kitt (additionally symbolic for being the first Black Catwoman) to the regal Grace Jones (who personifies art), both rightly play women who are either the face or the brains behind the company where Marcus works. While they both play parodies of themselves within overt sexualities, their magnificence – both in the real world and within scene-stealing performances – pales any belittling this film dares attempt.

As women heroes were hailed, they were also made. In a more conscious world, the additional love interest of wholesome newbie Halle Berry would've been a Meg Ryan rival and perhaps become the first Black woman to win an Oscar for something less harrowing than *Monster's Ball*. And by bringing in the lungs of an inconspicuous Toni Braxton, the *Boomerang* soundtrack was the beginning of her Grammy-laden career.

Boomerang's appreciation has ripened with time, as today's critics are more aware that Black lives matter; despite the movie being one of the most successful of 1992, it was referred to as a 'strangely retrograde Fantasyland' (to quote just one similarly obnoxious review) upon the inability to fathom a Black wealthy world.

OTHER ROMCOMS TO BINGE:

COMING TO AMERICA (1988)
Boomerang may be noted as the first Black cast studio romcom but there's a heavy dose of romance in this earlier classic comedy, also starring Eddie Murphy.

THE BEST MAN (1999, SEE PAGE 92)
Another nourishing reflection of a Black aspirational world within a cast of characters who enjoy talent, wealth and love.

EMPOWERED WOMEN WHO REFUSED TO SETTLE

SLEEPLESS IN SEATTLE

DIRECTOR: Nora Ephron
WRITERS: Nora Ephron, Jeff Arch, David S. Ward
YEAR: 1993

Blending old-school romance with eye-rolling cynicism, *Sleepless in Seattle* was a winning formula. But while this romcom staple has long been seen as the height of romantic lunacy, there's progression in the actions of Annie, who gave it all up for love.

Annie, along with every other woman in America, becomes obsessed with recently widowed Sam when his adorable wingman of a son calls a radio show to get his dad a date. Despite Annie being comfy with a man allergic to existence, she can't help but wonder if there's more to life than stability and a bedpan of antihistamines.

With shrewd observational style so emblematic of Nora Ephron, *Sleepless* riffed on the evolving gender politics of dating and the growing independence of women in the 1990s. As Sam struggles to think when he last dated since his wife passed ('seventy ... eight'?) his exasperated friend Jay explains how things have moved on. Recognizing how contemporary women enjoyed the liberty to be crass about their desires, 'pecs and a cute butt' is his answer to Sam's wide-eyed curiosity. 'The good news is you get to split the cheque' is a brighter observation, not that Sam could imagine letting a woman pay for dinner, which Jay says will make him 'man of the year'.

But all that was just talk. Annie is the one who really brings women up to date by employing the options women had in the pursuit of love. While Sam's stopgap girlfriend Victoria represents the old-school method of waiting for a man to call, all Annie's waiting for is her dial-up internet so she can hire a detective to track Sam down. OK, stalking is never cool and is illegal for good reason, but at least Annie helped to level the romcom field where creepy men were rife.

Whatever you think of Annie's wooing methods, there's romanticism at heart, and it's Hollywood (and specifically the 1957 classic *An Affair to Remember*) that has perpetuated such lofty ideals. Yet, considering many women of the 1950s may have had to marry into financial security, Annie represented the 1990s affluent woman (when journalism paid the bills) who could support herself if it didn't work out.

OTHER ROMCOMS TO BINGE:

AN AFFAIR TO REMEMBER (1957)
If only to pay respect to the source material.

YOU'VE GOT MAIL (1998, SEE PAGE 80)
Another Nora Ephron classic where her leading lady gives it all up for love (overlooking the fact she probably could have done better).

HE'S JUST NOT THAT IN TO YOU (2009)
Basic advice from a basic romcom: maybe don't settle for someone who's not worth your time.

DECONSTRUCTED THE FAIRYTALE WEDDING

MURIEL'S WEDDING

DIRECTOR: P.J. Hogan
WRITER: P.J. Hogan
YEAR: 1994

The poster for *Muriel's Wedding* is deceiving. Judging from the big grin on Muriel's face and her even bigger white dress, you'd think you were looking at the outcome of another run-of-the-mill romcom. Yet it's a gleeful dark comedy about how women are sold a marriage fantasy and, for those who settled in to have their idea of an idyllic wedding spit-polished, it may have been a wake-up call. In this 1990s classic that gave us the catchphrase, 'You're terrible, Muriel,' marriage isn't a means to an end - best friends and ABBA songs are.

Muriel's Wedding quickly gets to work on making that fairytale wedding a pipe dream when the nuptials it opens on are followed by the groom banging a bridesmaid. But Muriel, with her pre-Pinterest shrine to bridal dresses on her wall, still sees marriage as an escape from her coastal town of Porpoise Spit and dysfunctional family – especially her politician-wannabe father who's cheating on her mother Betty. Betty may mope around in between preparing cups of tea in the microwave, but she makes one of the film's gnarliest points: sometimes, marriage isn't just miserable, it's tragic.

When Muriel finds herself in Sydney, she finds a new friend in Rhonda to belt out ABBA karaoke and gush over how marriage will make her 'a new person'. But it's when Rhonda combats Muriel's Barbie-like frenemies with the line 'I'm not alone, I'm with Muriel' that we know *this* is the relationship that will turn her life around.

In between the camp comedy, which sees Rhonda and Muriel cackle through disastrous dates, and Muriel's sham wedding to an Olympic South African swimmer who needs a green card (because, initially, Muriel really is that desperate), the film reflects on how the changing of the last name, the puffy dress, the wedding cake under the pillow and catching the bouquet are all fanciful rituals only fed to women. Besides, who's going to clean those pillowcases? Exactly.

And yet the movie doesn't give up on love and the transformative effect of finding your person. In puritan romcom style, Rhonda and Muriel make a break for the airport and drive into the sunset, leaving us on a sugary high. Thanks to Rhonda, Muriel finally sees that she's not so terrible after all.

OTHER ROMCOMS TO BINGE:

THELMA & LOUISE (1991)
Muriel driving off into the sunset with her new best friend is definitely inspired by this greatest film of female solidarity.

MAMMA MIA! (2008, SEE PAGE 134)
Where a last-minute U-turn at the altar was music to her ears.

STRICTLY BALLROOM (1992)
Another heightened, camp Australian romance.

GAVE US THE FEMINIST
FASHIONISTA

CLUELESS

DIRECTOR: Amy Heckerling
WRITER: Amy Heckerling
YEAR: 1995

In 1995's *Clueless*, the eclectic (and computerized) wardrobe of our heroine Cher (Alicia Silverstone) provides an arsenal of agency. Across 60 outfit changes, *Clueless* is a witty observation of how coming-of-age feminists in the 1990s simultaneously embraced unapologetic femininity and righteous girl-power.

From that sunny yellow plaid outfit to the layering of crop tops, Cher presented someone who loved fashion and the self-esteem it inspired, while capitalizing on the few powers afforded to her as a young sexualized woman. *Clueless'* wardrobe designer Mona May talked of leaning into femininity at a time when 1990s fashion was all about grunge. 'I've always felt femininity is so important for girls to express with confidence.' Even using the excuse of 'riding the crimson wave', to explain being late to class, was a savvy use of Cher's body in an unblushing reference to menstruation in conservative mainstream Hollywood.

Cher, her best friend Dionne and later her love interest Christian, the 'Streisand ticket holdin' friend of Dorothy' (aka gay), provided catharsis for those who loved playing dress-up but considered it a guilty pleasure. And while the romcom makeover trope gets many an eye-roll, here it's a power move claiming it gave Cher 'a sense of control in a world full of chaos'. As for

Cher and Dionne's 'project' of reinventing new girl Tai, it's far less demeaning considering it serves as a meaningful female friendship and not just some guy. After all, it's Cher's kinship with her fellow girls that makes this movie thrive, as they explore their new powers of womanhood and individuality through a shared love of style.

Cher as a clueless bimbo? *As if!* Refreshingly, Heckerling's script – with the whip-smart energy of Jane Austen's *Emma* – doesn't equate her preoccupation with style to an insufficiency of brains. Instead, she's ambitious and compassionate, and, like any naturally naive 16-year-old, skips from clanging moments of ignorance – 'You know I don't speak Mexican' – to mic-drop moments of wisdom: 'There's no RSVP on the statue of Liberty!' Speaking to *Vice* magazine in 2016, Heckerling claimed, 'I didn't want [Cher] to be not intelligent, I wanted her to just not know what she didn't know yet.'

OTHER ROMCOMS TO BINGE:

LEGALLY BLONDE (2001, SEE PAGE 106)
Serious about her fashion. Serious about getting into Harvard Law School. 'What? Like it's hard?'

EMMA (2020)
Another fruity rendition of the source material.

SEX AND THE CITY (2008, SEE PAGE 136)
No one embraced the catharsis of capitalism more than Carrie Bradshaw, who only uses her oven as somewhere to store more clothes.

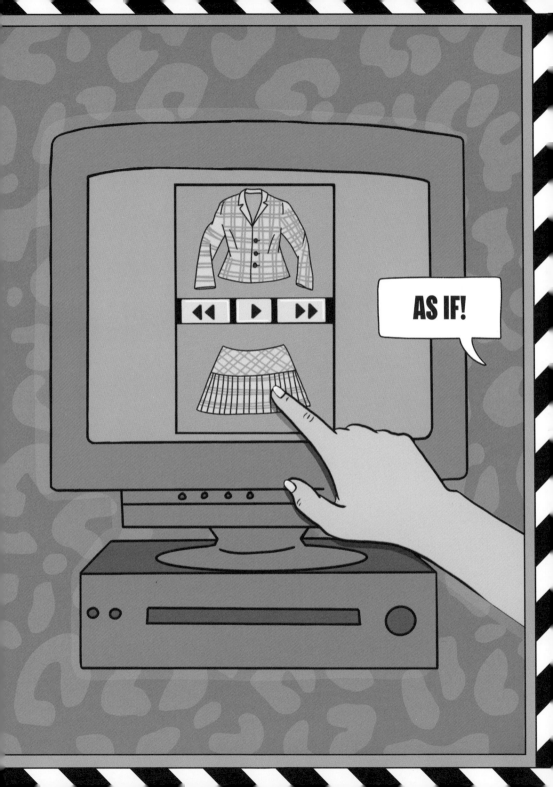

VALIDATED THE EMOTIONS OF BLACK WOMEN

WAITING TO EXHALE

DIRECTOR: Forest Whitaker
WRITERS: Terry McMillan, Ron Bass
YEAR: 1995

When Queen Latifah's character in *Brown Sugar* tells her friend Syd that she's becoming a Terry McMillan character, it's a nod of deep respect. It came as her emotions were reaching new depth, while blossoming for us to behold. When McMillan's third book *Waiting to Exhale* went on to become the groundbreaking romcom it is, Black women were given both liberating visibility and a licence to feel.

Bernadine, Gloria, Savannah and Robin are all successful in their own way but miss the love they deserve, and as they hold their breath to feel something real, their inner monologue expresses their doubt. Despite thriving careers and beautiful homes, we hear how they are their own best friend and worst enemy as they navigate life. Bernadine would 'clone herself but wouldn't have time for the surgery', while Robin who 'likes pretty boys with big sticks' consistently makes excuses for subpar men. Savannah's disappointing sexual encounters have her wishing she just 'had a V8', and Gloria's New Year's resolution of losing '10, no 15 – OK ... 35 pounds' makes her just as relatable.

While much of this insight has us chuckling with solidarity, it is an accessory to the more salient emotions that Black women are often denied. Through unbridled joy, triumphant success and the appreciation of a Black female gaze (Wesley Snipes has never looked finer),

each woman contributes to the dynamism of humanity that isn't just pain.

But it's anger that's presented as most significantly freeing. In a world where the 'angry Black woman' has become a racist trope, anger is liberated by a spectrum of very valid rage – from being objectified or undermined (as Robin and Savannah frequently are), to acting up because you're heartbroken (as Gloria is when her son leaves home). Then there's the simple fact that life just isn't fair (especially when you fall for a married or gay man). But Bernadine's fury is the one that really burns bright. As she struts from her cheating husband's burning car, her arson summons the fire of a thousand suns, creating the perfect meme for when revenge is sweet.

With McMillan's winning formula making box-office success, she paved the way for honest, vulnerable and human Black female representations. And for Black women exhausted by respectability politics or code-switching through life, *Waiting to Exhale* provided invigorating room to breathe.

OTHER ROMCOMS TO BINGE:

GIRLS TRIP (2017, SEE PAGE 170)
Yet another example of how successful films can be when Black female friendships take the lead.

HOW STELLA GOT HER GROOVE BACK (1998, SEE PAGE 78)
Another Terry McMillan banger, with Angela Bassett finding that groove.

LEFT PRINCE CHARMING
AT THE ALTAR

WHILE YOU WERE SLEEPING

DIRECTOR: Jon Turteltaub
WRITERS: Daniel G. Sullivan, Fredric Lebow
YEAR: 1995

Disney's bread and butter has historically told girls they will find a Prince Charming – a hope that has also clung to the hand of love at first sight. But thanks to Sandra Bullock's endearing 1990s romcom, this irresponsible myth was sweetly blown apart.

While You Were Sleeping is a movie about 'falling in love at second sight' and finding someone real (and preferably conscious). It sees lonely, orphaned transit worker Lucy turn princess in shining armour when she rescues handsome Peter from an oncoming train. Lucy's never properly met Peter, but she'd been admiring her 'Prince Charming' from afar and now here he is: in her arms and slipping into a coma on Christmas Day. With the gift of survival being up there with the best Christmas presents of all, it's only fair she gets what she's always wanted in return ...

Let's not be too harsh on what she does next. Of course, masquerading as his fiancée is pretty daft – even for the age-old romcom custom of flirting with farce. But to subvert the *Sleeping Beauty* plot (which has always been creepy) there's a power play to Lucy claiming her comatose catch.

As Mr Perfect (a deliberately Disneyesque Peter Gallagher) lies unconscious, his big adorable family gobbles up the idea that he and Lucy are due to be wed. The more she

becomes attached to the prospect of belonging to this unit, the less she does to correct them until, plot twist, she meets Peter's brother Jack. While sparks begin to fly, Lucy's so far down the aisle that she's almost marrying Peter. But when he wakes up and says, 'My family love ya, so I might as well love ya,' he's hardly a match for Jack, who's actually earned her love. In a move that sees her triumphantly object to her own wedding, Lucy rewrites her own happily ever after with Jack, who still comes as a package with the family she's grown to love.

We'd be here all day if we picked apart the plausibility of this premise, so let's focus on the message that Prince Charming doesn't exist and Cinderella can do better. Besides, finding 'The One' doesn't equate to happiness – that comes with family, community and sharing a love that loves you back.

OTHER ROMCOMS TO BINGE:

SPEED (1994)
A romcom in disguise with Bullock at the wheel.

SOUL FOOD (1997)
Marriage is a family affair around the dinner table of this big ensemble.

SLIDING DOORS (1998)
Imagine if Lucy didn't manage to roll Peter off the tracks – now, that would be a sinister (and shorter) movie. The quintessential 'what if' romance.

MADE SINGLE WORKING MOTHERS FEEL SEEN

ONE FINE DAY

DIRECTOR: Michael Hoffman
WRITERS: Terrel Seltzer, Ellen Simon
YEAR: 1996

With many romcoms concentrating on young love, here in hard-nosed 1990s corporate America was a grown-up modern romance gem. One that understood that single women with kids are still desirable and that divorce or being over 30 doesn't make you undatable. Of course, it helps if you look like George Clooney or Michelle Pfeiffer, but we are here to dream.

One Fine Day sees two divorced parents tackle a day in the office while juggling childcare. Worlds collide when Jack (George Clooney) fails to get his daughter to meet Melanie (Michelle Pfeiffer) so they can get their kids to a school trip in time. As they literally miss the boat, our newly met enemies reluctantly cobble something together to survive the day in a way that would make 24's Jack Bauer proud.

Here's a romcom that truly understands the amorphous shape of a day for those who have young kids. From doing life admin and feeding herself after putting her son to bed, to waking up in the night because he's thirsty, Melanie makes single mothers feel seen. And while she's perfectly capable of raising her child alone, the film strikes a respectful balance with someone who perhaps would rather not.

Before flexible working, this film hinted at the concept by demonstrating the boundaries parents with additional jobs need. When Melanie uses her multitasking skills to smash her presentation, she's eventually clear that she'd rather get to her son's soccer game than stay for celebration martinis. And amen for her genuine desire to do so. In a ditch full of depictions of the horror of motherhood, here is a woman not regretting her life choices while demonstrating how hard parenting is. For mothers who don't have an additional job, *One Fine Day* sees you too. When her sister brazenly reminds her, 'I do work, I am the CEO of this household,' Michelle's self-importance gets a gentle release of air.

One Fine Day best exemplifies the unexpected timings of a parent's day by placing its makeover scene at the end. After succumbing to Jack's charms and freshening up 'so I feel like a woman and not a dead mommy', Melanie leaves her bathroom to see an equally exhausted George Clooney asleep on her sofa. What more could you want from a happily ever after?

OTHER ROMCOMS TO BINGE:

BABY BOOM (1987, SEE PAGE 42)
Another workplace vs motherhood battle that settled on a draw.

CLAUDINE (1974, SEE PAGE 38)
Claudine has 99 problems (six kids and unstable welfare cheques being some) but dating James Earl Jones ain't one.

SHONE LIGHT ON BLACK LESBIAN LOVE

THE WATERMELON WOMAN

DIRECTOR: Cheryl Dunye
WRITERS: Cheryl Dunye, Douglas McKeown
YEAR: 1996

Whatever it is you're looking for in *The Watermelon Woman* – be it a sexy 1990s romcom or an investigative jab at the politics of Black women's representation – you'll get more than you bargained for in this innovative gem. Behold, the self-titled 'Dunyementary': a layered cake of fiction, documentary, autobiography and romantic comedy lovingly iced by Cheryl Dunye, the woman behind the first narrative feature to be directed by an out Black lesbian.

Meet Cheryl (played by Liberian-American Dunye): a cool, cute, lesbian film-maker from Philly who wants to find out more about 'The Watermelon Woman' – a Black actress simply credited as such in a 1930s film. But Cheryl's film aims not just to unearth the story behind this mystery woman, but also to ask the wider, more pressing question of why 'Black women's stories never get told'.

Along the way, we hang out with quippy fellow-lesbian best-friend Tamara, see some blind-date clangers (never attempt Minnie Riperton's 'Lovin' You' at karaoke) and are entwined in a sultry romance with Diana – an artsy white woman that Cheryl meets while working at a video-rental store. After a hard day of digging around archives, interviewing friends and family, and visiting the Center for Lesbian Information

and Technology (yes, that spells 'CLIT'), the alluring Diana offers some VHS and chill.

In a field barren of representations of Black and interracial lesbian lovers, the lovemaking scene alone is enough to give *The Watermelon Woman* a revolutionary zing. Ending the invisibility of women who look like Dunye, here she put herself in the picture where other films hadn't dared. In this organic, radical act of just portraying her truth, she opened up the world of titillation, away from the straight gratuitous gaze.

In this seminal example of ambidextrous film-making (not to mention a homage to rad 1990s fashion), Dunye nimbly juggles romance, political satire and mockumentary to flick the lights on for Black lesbians in love. And although the plot itself is a work of fiction, the real story of how hard it is to uncover the lives of historical Black women – period – is a very real work of art. Dunye's right: sometimes you have to create your own history.

OTHER ROMCOMS TO BINGE:

GO FISH (1994)
Led by Guinevere Turner (*The Watermelon Woman*'s Diana), this sensitive lesbian romcom is one for the ages.

THE INCREDIBLY TRUE ADVENTURE OF TWO GIRLS IN LOVE (1995)
An indie gem that broaches interracial dating between two sweet-hearted girls.

CENTRED A BLACK WOMAN'S LOVE, NOT PAIN

LOVE JONES

DIRECTOR: Theodore Witcher
WRITER: Theodore Witcher
YEAR: 1997

In the Criterion DVD edition of *Love Jones's* director's commentary, Theodore Witcher points out a scene he wanted cut. It's the point where lovers Nina and Darius are rekindling their romance by running through a park. Confessing to Larenz Tate (who plays the love-struck Darius) that he thought it was too 'cheesy', Tate made a point that convinced him to keep it in: 'We don't even get cheesy, let it play.' Tate had made a valid point, as in 1997 Black romcoms were so rare that they hadn't yet reached the luxury of being formulaic.

The 1990s was a golden age for Black Hollywood, but the decade was marred with themes of gangsters, death or pain. Even 1995's progressive *Waiting to Exhale* saw its four women deal with shattered hearts. But in *Love Jones*, we see an autonomous Black woman receive sex, love and joy in a film where no one dies. As this low bar is hurdled with trailblazing success, photographer Nina makes a first move on poet Darius. After an on-stage freestyle of his sex-charged poem, Nina reminds him that 'there are other topics' and writes 'love' on his hand before coolly walking away. In this perfectly formed scene we know where we stand – on the brink of a rare story that centres Black romance.

We soon witness her feelings evolve from lust to love. When her friend digs for details of her and Darius's first night, Nina says, 'It was like his dick just … talked to me,' while lit up with giggles. One day impulsive, another poker-faced cool, Nina keeps us guessing as much as she keeps Darius on his toes.

We can thank *Love Jones* for a wake of vulnerable, soulful, capricious Black women leads. Think Sanaa Lathan in *Love & Basketball* and *Brown Sugar*, or any woman in *The Best Man*. And taking Nina's essence, right down to her photographic talents, Issa Rae in *The Photograph* is a gold-star ode. Yet, it's a roll call still short against a majority of white romcoms, and that cheesy utopia is still frustratingly out of reach.

OTHER ROMCOMS TO BINGE:

MEDICINE FOR MELANCHOLY (2008)
This dreamy Barry Jenkins' debut is 24 hours of pure infatuation as Micah (Wyatt Cenac) spends a day with the girl from the night before.

THE PHOTOGRAPH (2020)
Issa Rae and LaKeith Stanfield positively sizzle in this gorgeous, electric romance lit up with their chemistry.

RYE LANE (2023, SEE PAGE 212)
Thanks to a resurging kick from Vivian Oparah, the romcom is alive and well, and living in Brixton.

SHOWED BEING IRRATIONAL WAS JUST A RITE OF PASSAGE

MY BEST FRIEND'S WEDDING

DIRECTOR: P.J. Hogan
WRITER: Ron Bass
YEAR: 1997

In the earlier era of the romantic comedy, the key ingredient to the genre's success was to provide a happy ending. Come 1997, however, and audiences were on a sugar crash and possibly still brushing their teeth after being told 'you complete me' by Jerry Maguire. Suddenly, the market was open for something a little less saccharine.

We're of course talking about the revolutionary anti-heroine of Jules (Julia Roberts), who commits grand theft auto, smokes, sends fraudulent emails and does bad things to good people, like sabotaging the wedding of her best friend Mike because she's decided he should be marrying her instead.

This irrational behaviour isn't completely crazy if you consider that 27-year-old Jules is responding to the pressures placed on women nudging 30. Her blood oath with Mike to marry each other at the ancient age of 28 if they've not yet met The One is just one of the many idolized romantic notions the film ridicules. Another is the hyper-kitsch opening number of Hal David and Burt Bacharach's, 'Wishin' and Hopin'', which lovingly harks back to 1950s romcom openers such as *Pillow Talk* and *Artists and Models*.

Director P.J. Hogan (fresh from marriage-mockery masterpiece *Muriel's Wedding*) and writer Ron Bass (whom we have to thank for the empowering *How Stella Got Her Groove Back*) gave us a film that turned the romcom heroine on its pretty little head. Jules showed women how literally chasing a Disneyfied version of a man who leads you on isn't a happy ending, and that doing anything for love – as many romcoms might lead us to believe – isn't romantic, but silly. Just ask Kimmy, who quits architecture school to follow Mike around in an unstable job.

Turns out we were so ready for Jules, as in a test screening for an alternative ending, which sees her find love at the eleventh hour, audiences hated it. Perhaps they felt robbed of what ultimately is a more feminist conclusion – a woman who had always been, as Kimmy describes her, 'not up for anything conventional or popularly assumed to be female priorities. Including marriage'.

OTHER ROMCOMS TO BINGE:

PALM SPRINGS (2020, SEE PAGE 202)
To be fair, there's no such thing as being rational when you're stuck in a time loop with someone you love to hate.

WOMEN ON THE VERGE OF A NERVOUS BREAKDOWN (1988)
Bad behaviour (and spiked gazpacho) has never looked so glorious. From the consistently feminist auteur Pedro Almodóvar.

THE ROMCOM THAT...

FULFILLED A BLACK WOMAN'S SEXUAL DESIRE

HOW STELLA GOT HER GROOVE BACK

DIRECTOR: Kevin Rodney Sullivan
WRITERS: Terry McMillan, Ron Bass
YEAR: 1998

After the success of Terry McMillan's *Waiting to Exhale*, Hollywood realized Black women were woefully underserved. When her subsequent novel enjoyed more bestselling success, it was a no-brainer to bring it to the screen. And in her most autobiographical story yet, Stella (Angela Bassett) embodied her own experience of fulfilling her fantasy with a man half her age.

Stella is a hardened divorced stockbroker who could really do with letting off steam. When a trip to the spa barely buffs the surface, she books a trip to Jamaica on an uncharacteristic whim. Drafting in best friend Delilah (Whoopi Goldberg), along for the laughs, a young Winston Shakespeare (Taye Diggs) catches her eye. After a charismatic pursuit, she eventually believes him when he insists on how irrelevant their age difference is.

After decades of films that relished the 1980s and 1990s corporate toil, it was a vacation in itself to see a working woman relax. And as men were congratulated for dating below their age, Stella challenged the 'cougar' trope as a smart woman embracing choice. The story confronts preconceptions on how such an age gap is perceived (and then practically works within a relationship), and as we are strapped into the seat of Stella's lust, we get our kicks by enjoying her thirst. From the moment Winston joins her for breakfast, she drinks in the sight of his glistening silhouette. From the contours of a bicep to the crest of his lips, we're invited to join her as she dares to dream.

Sullivan tested newcomer Diggs' appeal among the Black women he knew to avoid his own assumptions on what they deemed hot. And by workshopping the love scenes directly with Bassett, he listened when she told him, 'It's my fantasy. HE needs to be naked, not me,' unlocking sex scenes from a woman's point of view.

Of course, we must respect there's more nuance to the sexual thirst of Black women, and that it certainly exists beyond heteronormative lust, but at a time when the representation of Black women's gaze was practically absent, here was a film that plucked lovingly from some juicy low-hanging fruit.

OTHER ROMCOMS TO BINGE:

LOVE JONES (1997, SEE PAGE 74)
Enjoy seeing Nia Long getting the service she deserves (and not just the cooked breakfast in the morning).

THE WATERMELON WOMAN (1996, SEE PAGE 72)
A rare and beautiful love scene through the eyes of a Black lesbian woman made this a revolution.

THE BEST MAN HOLIDAY (2013)
For *that* scene where the quartet of male leads synchronize dance to 'Can You Stand the Rain'? Chef's kiss.

SAW THE INTERNET AS BOTH
A GIFT AND A CURSE

YOU'VE GOT MAIL

DIRECTOR: Nora Ephron
WRITERS: Miklós László,
Nora Ephron, Delia Ephron
YEAR: 1998

For a brief moment in time, the dawn of the internet presented a dating utopia for women. A place where romantic potential could be judged by the content of the written exchange and not a quick swipe. More specifically, thanks to AOL, chat rooms could be a place for women to court from the safety of their own home and the comfort of their sweatpants.

To further romanticize the internet as a protective cyber-Cupid, using chat rooms to find lovers was shown to be empowering and efficient. Suddenly, we could zone in on parts of the population we most fancied and shepherd them into a pen of curated desire. It felt productive. It felt progressive. It felt that thing that women in society rarely feel: powerful and safe.

This twinkle in time was snatched up by Nora Ephron's *You've Got Mail*, released just two years after AOL was available to those who could afford dial-up – and mere months before Google was considered a verb. Even the title sang the praises of this new communication tool, as it lifted a banal notification to a saucy little wink. The opening scene demonstrates this thrilling new development as we see Kathleen Kelly (Meg Ryan) firing up the modem in her pyjamas as soon as her tech-sceptic boyfriend leaves for work. After meeting in the 'Over 30s'

chat room, 'Shop Girl' and 'NY152' have moved to the next step by emailing each other a volley of wistful prose.

But *You've Got Mail* was also a vision into the gutter, as 'NY152' – aka Tom Hanks as Joe Fox – was a warning for what catfishing could be. And despite this movie being too green to acknowledge the extent of today's online abuse, it was wise enough to nod to women dabbling in cybersex, with Kathleen's shop assistant admitting, 'I tried to have cybersex once but I kept getting a busy signal.'

So, here's to a time when a busy signal was our only gripe, as soon dick pics and online stalking brought a chainsaw to the playground that should've been safe. And as *You've Got Mail* was the first pop-culture introduction to online dating, it became a romcom that provided both optimism and caution to putting your love online.

OTHER ROMCOMS TO BINGE:

LOVE, SIMON (2018)
Where emails were the closet for this breakout gay romcom.

THE SHOP AROUND THE CORNER (1940)
Back when it was good old-fashioned pen and paper – the movie *You've Got Mail* is based on.

DESK SET (1957)
Katharine Hepburn channels the curiosity and anxieties of the evolving world of tech.

TAUGHT GIRLS YOU DON'T NEED TO CONFORM

10 THINGS I HATE ABOUT YOU

DIRECTOR: Gil Junger
WRITERS: Karen McCullah, Kirsten Smith, William Shakespeare
YEAR: 1999

With its many layers, *10 Things I Hate About You* is the feminist onion of the 1990s romcom. Smashing Shakespeare's *The Taming Of The Shrew* with third-wave feminist values, this punchy classic from the women writers behind *Legally Blonde* solidified the romcom trope of the girl who refuses to conform.

Meet Katarina Stratford: her sister Bianca says she's from 'planet loser' (and, by contrast, Bianca is from 'planet look at me, look at me') and the film soon shows how everyone at Padua High School obediently slots into some sort of tribe. But Kat dances to the beat of her own drum (or on the table, to The Notorious B.I.G.), much like fellow loner Patrick. No prizes for guessing how that turns out.

A glazed reading of our shrew Kat being tamed by Patrick (even if he was paid to date her) would miss one of the most revolutionary points that *10 Things* makes: succumbing to love doesn't make you weak when you've found someone who makes you stronger. And if he sings 'Can't Take My Eyes Off You' over the baseball field Tannoy? Then, yes, he can stay.

Kat embodies those who came of age in the 1990s and felt charged by a new tide of female empowerment. Her love of Bikini Kill punk rock, casual reading of *The Bell Jar* and recategorizing

of 'heinous bitch' to 'tempestuous' make it clear Kat has her claws out for societal structures.

But this film is wise beyond its years to know that one pretty white girl can't hold all the weight of a feminist deity. When her Black teacher calls 'Miss I Have An Opinion On Everything' out on her white feminism, mimicking how 'tough it must be to overcome suburban middle-class oppression', the film is telling us – as Mr Morgan is telling Kat – that race, class and gender must all be part of the feminist dialogue.

This romcom was a palate cleanser after the sour taste of *She's All That* (also released in 1999) and the spew of other films that saw women having to shed their skin in order to fit in (Sandy in *Grease* also has a lot to answer for). Instead, Kat was spared a gooey transformative prom-date makeover (she just threw on a dress – no biggie), stuck to her principles and didn't live up to anyone's expectations but her own.

OTHER ROMCOMS TO BINGE:

PLUS ONE (2019, SEE PAGE 194)
Alice (Maya Erskine) isn't playing by anyone's rules but her own.

LAGGIES (ALSO KNOWN AS 'SAY WHEN', 2014)
For complex, mischievous, stereotype-busting women, Lynn Shelton films are where it's at.

THE DUFF (2015)
This 'Designated Ugly Fat Friend' resists the urge to conform.

PROVED THERE'S NO ONE WAY TO BE GAY

BUT I'M A CHEERLEADER

DIRECTOR: Jamie Babbit
WRITERS: Jamie Babbit, Brian Peterson
YEAR: 1999

As the 1990s tipped into the 2000s, popular culture didn't hold back over its fetishization of cheerleaders. As the dynamic *Buffy the Vampire Slayer* slid into the less dimensional series of *Bring It On* movies, *American Beauty* brought us to a creepy brink of how far this obsession could go. But while most depictions served to quench a male gaze, Natasha Lyonne's Megan was here to cheer for an alternative team.

Sweet-as-pie Megan is an all-American girl. She aces her grades, loves cheerleading and has a handsome jock boyfriend who kisses her like a dog licks its bowl (because that's what straight couples do, right?) So why have her parents carted her off to a gay conversion camp? Sure, she has posters of girls in her locker, is partial to tofu and fantasizes about the up skirts of her fellow teammates, but she's a hyper-femme cheerleader so can't possibly be *whisper it* a *lesbian?*

But I'm A Cheerleader radicalized the genre of both romcoms and cheerleading films by plugging the subjective gaze into the eye sockets of a girl. While validating the thirst of a young girl's desire, it went further by cheering on ambiguous queer representation. Megan finds herself at True Directions conversion camp (ingeniously marshalled by a pre-*Drag Race* RuPaul in a very tight 'Straight Is Great' T-shirt) and is introduced to a community where no one person is the same. From butch, to bi, goth to grunge, the high-school tropes are lovingly ticked off with a rainbow-coloured pen. And when pretty blonde Megan falls for edgy, cool Graham (Clea DuVall), the message is clear that there is no one way to be gay.

The camp's efforts to pummel aggressive gender expectations into these teens is buoyed by the gaudy camp aesthetic that just makes it absurd. In reality such a place is no laughing matter and still legally operates in many US states. But in this cult classic, True Directions eventually becomes a place of joy, where found family and true love live. And as Megan's pom-poms pivot from football hunks to Graham, you can't help but be moved by her final cheer of declaration.

OTHER ROMCOMS TO BINGE:

EDGE OF SEVENTEEN (1998)
Because it was about time queer guys got their own cute coming of age romcom.

SAVED! (2004)
Less gay, more trying to fight chaste expectations of attending a strict religious high school.

THE MISEDUCATION OF CAMERON POST (2018)
Where putting a bunch of horny, queer teenagers in a conversion camp is, again, counterproductive.

HUMANIZED THE
HOLLYWOOD ACTOR

NOTTING HILL

DIRECTOR: Roger Michell
WRITER: Richard Curtis
YEAR: 1999

Notting Hill's meet-cute sees dusty book-lover Anna (Julia Roberts) bump into dusty bookshop-owner William (Hugh Grant), as they collide on the street in a coffee-spill catastrophe. As Will dissolves into his signature 'whoopsie daisy' mess, his bubbling verbal lava has him babbling something about a prostitute. It can be read as a nod to Roberts' fantastical role of Vivian in the astronomical hit *Pretty Woman*, but in the latte-lacquered streets of Notting Hill, she's more than a fetishized version of a sex worker. Here, she's 'just a girl, asking a boy to love her'.

The meta wiring of *Notting Hill* doesn't end there – this movie simply doesn't work without Julia Roberts being Julia Roberts. No need to pretend she's the most famous Hollywood star in the world because here she is, playing herself. In lines that twinkle with a knowing wink, Juli—Sorry, Anna Scott breathes humanity into the challenges that an actress in the tabloid-infested 1990s faced. Especially Roberts, who endured headlines like 'Pretty Fickle Woman' as a result of a merry-go-round love life.

In a dinner-party scene, a game of schadenfreude Top Trumps sees guests try to win the last brownie with their story of woe. It's here that Will's star-struck friends get a sobering insight into the challenges that Anna faces for just doing her job. We're talking the 10-year diet, the painful surgery and the numerous heartbreaks lived out in public. Later, her 'sex tape' further reveals the lose-lose situation of women in the spotlight.

OK, her life may not be as tough as Bella's (Gina McKee), who can't have kids after an accident left her wheelchair-bound, but come the credits we know how mentally difficult Anna's life is and the lengths she needs to go to just to stay sane.

The most empowering thing about Jul—Sorry, Anna, is that she never sacrifices her career and calls the shots in the courtship throughout. And in a figure that Roberts insisted was raised when Richard Curtis lowballed her in the script, she stiffly reveals how much she gets paid ($15m, btw). In a telling closing sequence, Anna expertly glides across a red carpet as Will awkwardly trips up. They may be together but he's going to have to keep up, as it's still her world – he's just living in it.

OTHER ROMCOMS TO BINGE:

MY WIFE IS AN ACTRESS (2001)
A comic embrace of fragile masculinity when paranoia plagues a man married to an actor. That actor? Charlotte Gainsbourg.

LA LA LAND (2016)
Maybe the fact that Emma Stone's character is undermined by Ryan Gosling is the very point being made about women in acting? Tell yourself that to enjoy it that bit more.

DID AWAY WITH THE 'BRIDEZILLA'

RUNAWAY BRIDE

DIRECTOR: Garry Marshall
WRITERS: Sara Parriott, Josann McGibbon
YEAR: 1999

Oversimplified assessments of gendered relationship roles have long been represented in two basic camps: the commitment-phobe man and the wedding-hungry woman. Yet, in 1999 – four years after the term 'bridezilla' was coined in a *Boston Globe* article – Maggie (Julia Roberts) turned the tables as she ran backwards down the aisle.

The clue's in the title on where this premise goes, but here we get three cold-feet fiascos before our heroine finally says 'I do'. As we meet Maggie, who is fresh from fleeing on horseback from yet another ditched wedding, we also meet Ike – a *USA Today* journalist who's accepted the accusation that his column 'traffics in female stereotypes'. While guilty, he's not sorry, and with slimy redemption he aims to prove his point by covering what he's coined 'the man eater'.

As Ike's investigation unravels the cause of Maggie's wedding allergy, *Runaway Bride*'s writers (Sara Parriott and Josann McGibbon in one of Hollywood's lengthiest writing partnerships) make sure this is no knight-in-shining-armour story. In a touching moment with her best friend Peggy, Maggie is confronted about flirting with her husband, in a firm but fair scene. With zero judgement and with no claws out, we see how strong female friendships are able to point out each other's destructive flaws.

Across her failed weddings, we learn how Maggie has just become used to going with the flow but, in a significant point about how she likes her eggs, finding real love helps her make decisions for herself. Seeing as someone has finally asked, she loves eggs Benedict and hates 'big weddings with everyone staring' – and, fresh with the vigour of finally knowing who she is, it's her who pops the question in the most earnest of ways. As for that fourth wedding? It's as wholesome as fresh bread, and no men were eaten as a result of this big but humble day.

OTHER ROMCOMS TO BINGE:

PRIVATE BENJAMIN (1980)
More altar-ditching scenes from Goldie Hawn in a wedding dress.

IT HAPPENED ONE NIGHT (1934, SEE PAGE 20)
The original and best wedding-day change of heart.

IT HAD TO BE YOU (1947)
It's fourth time lucky too for Ginger Roger's character, who has a habit of running away from the groom.

EXPLORED THE EQUALITY OF A THROUPLE ON HER TERMS

SPLENDOR

DIRECTOR: Gregg Araki
WRITERS: Gregg Araki, Jill Cargerman
YEAR: 1999

Traditionally, love triangles point to trouble, and polyandry gets you arrested. As for the verdict on whether you can love more than one person at a time, the jury's still out. Love beyond the nuclear family scenario has long seen us clutching our pearls, but in this overlooked gem of a punk romantic comedy, the concept of a throuple is more practical than perverse.

In a departure from his angst-ridden cult movies that pioneered a new wave of queer cinema, potent director Gregg Araki was ready to zhuzh up the romcom. Underneath his former dark material, Araki was a secret romcom connoisseur who appreciated the genre's power to dismantle traditional representations of love.

Cosying up to those familiar romcom beats, struggling actress Veronica and her lesbian best friend Mike attend a fancy dress party where she has two meet-cutes for the price of one. While Zed is a thickly sliced 'He-Man', Abel fulfils the adorably clumsy woman trope in the progressive shape of an effeminate man. After some comedic negotiations, they end up cohabiting under one roof, telling us that 'as demented as our relationship seemed to the outside world ... it worked'.

It feels triumphant to see a woman we're rooting for lavished with so much love. Beyond the lovemaking, which sees them prioritize her

pleasure, 'Beavis and Butt-Head' muck in around the house and provide emotional support. When the curveball of pregnancy and a third man threatens to topple the triangle, Zed and Abel unite to prove their love and willingness to work as a tripod. Ending on a scene that will awaken any weary new mother's fantasy, they squabble like big brothers over who gets to hold the baby.

If romantic comedies are the arena for a spectrum of romantic representations, people in three-way relationships should get their dues. Here we see unconventional happiness in an unconventional way, giving us a welcome provocation of monogamy norms. Valid complex human emotions aside, in a world where women are disproportionately left managing the home and family, maybe a trio provides more equality than we thought. Then again, maybe it just proves it takes two men to do one woman's work.

OTHER ROMCOMS TO BINGE:

DESIGN FOR LIVING (1933)
Splendor's exact premise, but with the romcom connoisseur touch of Ernst Lubitsch.

SHE'S GOTTA HAVE IT (1986, SEE PAGE 40)
Barely any films centre women within open relationships (let alone Black women), making this Spike Lee joint a rare gem.

JULES AND JIM (1962)
Where Jules, Jim and Catherine make up François Truffaut's love triangle.

TOOK NO WOMAN
FOR GRANTED

THE BEST MAN

DIRECTOR: Malcolm D. Lee
WRITER: Malcolm D. Lee
YEAR: 1999

The heyday of 1990s Black-cast romcoms ended with a surge of testosterone. Perhaps to find equilibrium with the women at large within Terry McMillan blockbusters *Waiting to Exhale* and *How Stella Got Her Groove Back*, or maybe to soothe an otherwise menacing representation of Black men after a decade of profitable gangster movies.

As the title suggests, *The Best Man* was aimed at the guys, so it's fair to accept that the women don't exactly lead. But collectively, within their brevity and within five individual personalities, they serve to remind us that no woman should be taken for granted.

Exhibit A is Jordan, whose nose for business would see her chastised in lesser romcom universes. And her aspirational attitude also applies to her lust when she propositions Harper to finish what they started in college. Then there's shy Candy, who enters the stag-do as the obligatory stripper. After leaving later in the night, we realize she lives by Audre Lorde's philosophy: 'If I didn't define myself, I would be crunched into other people's fantasies for me and eaten alive' – an intellect that cinematic sex workers are rarely afforded.

But it's bride-to-be Mia who really turns the tables when her angelic light dims to deliciously dark. She's the quiet anchor in this sea of big personalities, who happens to have a vengeful streak. In one lustful night that she'll take to her grave she squares her fiancé's infidelities privately with herself. Some may not believe in 'an eye for an eye' but to further stir the pot of dramatic irony, it's right there in the Bible that her fiancé holds close.

In a cigar-sucking chat around a boozy poker table, we hear the guys generalize the women in alpha-male tongues. Yet, one by one, the women break free from such summaries, making them all the better for proving them wrong.

OTHER ROMCOMS TO BINGE:

THE BEST MAN HOLIDAY (2013)
The year writer/director Malcolm D. Lee became the Black Santa Claus when he got the band back together for a festive revival.

THE BEST MAN: THE FINAL CHAPTERS (2022)
The TV series finale is where the women really pop (thanks to the insistence of writer/producer Dayna Lynne North).

PHANTOM THREAD (2017, SEE PAGE 172)
Never trust a big breakfast and a smile. That girl is poison.

HAD HER AMBITION
COME FIRST

LOVE & BASKETBALL

DIRECTOR: Gina Prince-Bythewood
WRITER: Gina Prince-Bythewood
YEAR: 2000

When writer/director Gina Prince-Bythewood told *The Hollywood Reporter* she wanted to make 'a Black *When Harry Met Sally*', she sold herself short. Sure, this set out her intention of replicating the unsurpassable battle of the sexes with an all-Black cast, but with *Love & Basketball* she erected a new plinth for the ambitious romcom heroine.

Set over four quarters, in an ode to its basketball stage, Monica (Sanaa Lathan) and Quincy (Omar Epps) are the kids next-door. While their slam-dunk talents excel to professional sporting status, their love of the court grows with that of each other.

What's acute in this love letter to both basketball (Prince-Bythewood herself is a former ball player) and Black love is how the battle-of-the-sexes plot thickens in the arena of sports. As well as battling the misogyny that fails to take female athletes seriously, motherhood and menstrual cycles are additional balls to dribble. Tenacious and wise, Monica's aware of the systems against her and as she's faced with breaking an all-important training curfew or tending to Quincy, who's in need of emotional support, it's a choice of tough love when she puts her ambition first.

It's a *Sliding Doors* moment that has Quincy feeling sore but, although compassionate to his feelings, she doesn't combust with regret. As their careers, alternative love lives and respective glass ceilings are met – not to mention Monica's navigation of what idealized femininity for a sportswoman is – we see the vulnerability of a woman trying to stay strong.

Monica provides a spritz of nuance to a woman facing a choice between love and ambition. In a gift to driven women everywhere, *Love & Basketball* says: have both, but know it will be hard-won. Sacrifices are made and hearts are broken, but in a 'double or nothing' twist with a heart-stopping one-on-one play-off for each other's heart, the eve of Quincy's wedding becomes the start of their next chapter.

Monica might get her happily ever after but through the prism of a story that centres a Black woman's dreams, Prince-Bythewood's fairytale ending is a comforting break from the norm.

OTHER ROMCOMS TO BINGE:

BEYOND THE LIGHTS (2014)
Another Gina Prince-Bythewood banger with Gugu Mbatha-Raw feeling the heat of a pop-star spotlight.

A LEAGUE OF THEIR OWN (1992)
More sporting ambition contending with gender norms. This time with Geena Davis swinging the bat.

BROWN SUGAR (2002, SEE PAGE 110)
Sanaa Lathan once again up top as a successful woman in hip-hop facing decisions of the heart.

TAUGHT WOMEN THE NEED FOR SELF-DEFENCE

MISS CONGENIALITY

DIRECTOR: Donald Petrie
WRITERS: Marc Lawrence, Katie Ford, Caryn Lucas
YEAR: 2000

Miss Congeniality presents Gracie Hart (Sandra Bullock) as a self-deprecating, workaholic cop whose disregard for feminine beauty ideals seems to leave her lonely. But if you assume her assignment of going undercover as a beauty queen gets her a guy and sees her live happily ever after, you'll overlook the journey that sees Gracie find not her femininity, but her feminism.

At first, Gracie is as misogynistic as her cocksure cop colleagues. She looks down on the women she has to compete alongside in the beauty pageant, snorting, 'Any woman that does this is catering to misogynistic Neanderthal mentality.' But as macho Gracie learns to walk in the beauty queens' high-heeled shoes (a vision Ellen DeGeneres claims she inspired, after the film's writers saw her learning to walk in a dress), she discovers their humanity and her own sisterhood.

The fauxmance between Eric (Benjamin Bratt) and Gracie has as much spark as a wet firework and that's exactly the point. It's a decoy to the blossoming love between Gracie and her fellow beauty queens – and, more specifically, Cheryl, aka Miss Rhode Island (Heather Burns).

With compassion comes protectiveness and, on a tipsy night out, Cheryl confesses she was attacked by a professor, shrugging the episode off as something that 'happens all the time'. Gracie, horrified, now realizes she must use her powers to protect her fellow women. Using the 'S.I.N.G.' acronym – 'Solar plexus, instep, nose and groin!' – she delivers a punchy self-defence class which is televised to women across America.

The popularity of women's self-defence classes has risen with each wave of feminism, starting with the suffragettes who had to learn how to fight against the police. It raises all sorts of questions about how threatened men felt and how women were becoming more aware of their physical strength. The importance of 'S.I.N.G' is brought home again when it appears in the sequel *Miss Congeniality 2: Armed and Fabulous*. As for Gracie's love life? Eric is conveniently written out, while Cheryl is back and ready to be saved by her queen in shining armour (because, yes, this is definitely a secret lesbian love affair winking from backstage).

OTHER ROMCOMS TO BINGE:

PROMISING YOUNG WOMAN (2020)
Carey Mulligan as a one-woman vigilante against male predators might be the opposite of romantic, but there's comic relief in her black-comedy heart.

PALM SPRINGS (2020, SEE PAGE 202)
Cristin Milioti's Sarah puts up a hell of a fight when she finds herself in Groundhog Day turmoil.

HIGHLIGHTED WOMEN'S ECONOMIC EMPOWERMENT

WHAT WOMEN WANT

DIRECTOR: Nancy Meyers
WRITERS: Josh Goldsmith,
Cathy Yuspa, Diane Drake
YEAR: 2000

In a romcom that could have been renamed 'What Audiences Want', this film drew in the masses and, with a box office of $374.1m, the Nancy Meyers blockbuster carried the romcom into the millennium. We'll have to accept that the 2000s was a simpler time for mainstream films' have-a-go feminism, as – by presenting a promotion as a way to prevent suicide, pretending to be gay as a fair way to dump someone and linking having a showgirl mother to the root of being chauvinist – *What Women Want* is often quite the opposite.

That aside, the film addresses the rising economic power of women at a time when glass ceilings were beginning to crack. Set in the grandiose offices of a huge marketing company, Nick cockily awaits his promotion to creative director. But then his boss acknowledges it's now a 'woman's world' and so hires the esteemed Darcy, who'd be far greater at tapping into the fact that 'female-driven advertising totalled $40 billion last year'. It's a point made throughout when they go after the Nike account: they workshop ideas based on more realistic women – something Nike oversaw and cast their real-life women CEOs.

The gift and the curse of Nick's ability to read women's minds is then used to steal Darcy's winning ideas – but this isn't the movie being sexist and rather a commentary on workplace sexism still going on today. While highlighting the boom in women's independent incomes, it touches on how this is only possible when career paths are accessible. Sure Darcy's promotion buys her a plush new pad, but when Nick steals her job, the fragility of her wealth is exposed, as she quickly has to sell.

With a cheerful promise of answering such a rhetorical question in a very binary world, *What Women Want* beckoned women in with the suggestion of being heard. Meanwhile, men could grab a pen and find out for themselves, especially if they were looking for women who were rich, white and did yoga. While that success is debatable, another is cold fact: women used their disposable income to make this one of the most successful films of the year. And in proving women-empowered films really do make bank, Meyers once again kept the romcom alight.

OTHER ROMCOMS TO BINGE:

WHAT MEN WANT (2019)
For the lols, you may as well watch the Black female version of this preposterous plot about reading the opposite sex's mind.

THE DEVIL WEARS PRADA (2006)
Few things celebrate the disposable income of women more than the world of high-fashion magazines.

GAVE US THE 'STRONG FEMALE INTROVERT'

AMÉLIE

DIRECTOR: Jean-Pierre Jeunet
WRITERS: Guillaume Laurant, Jean-Pierre Jeunet
YEAR: 2001

From the 'strong female character' to the girl who dances like no one's watching, the women of romcoms are often defined by their noise (just ask Meg Ryan). Of course, the medium of film is a stage for big characters, but what about representations of women who'd rather live life on the low? Chances are they come off as frigid, lonely or emo – if they even get to be a lead at all – but admiringly, Audrey Tautou helped to revise those labels with her exquisite portrayal of an introvert in love.

Amélie is our ingénue who lives in 1997 Paris, and in her head. She may not say much but she has the imagination of a child, as gloriously articulated through cinematic vignettes. On the backdrop of Princess Diana's tragic death (perhaps in ode to the most famous introvert of them all), Amélie flirts with an equally curious man by posting coded notes around town.

In this film, which went on to be one of the most successful French films ever, there are refreshing dynamics to the demeanour of an introvert; shy doesn't equate to a pushover, and quiet doesn't mean sexually reserved – and her reasons for being an introvert are afforded enlightening depth. As Amélie's backstory builds, we learn she's no virgin, but she has yet to find a man who can satisfy her more than cracking

the top of a crème brûlée. Thanks to her strong sense of justice, she defends others and herself with small acts of vengeance that remind us she's 'nobody's little weasel'.

'Whimsical' and 'quirky' are platitudes that an overwhelming amount of critics have used in their Amélie reviews, which says a lot about how we define women on film. Quiet, romantic men are 'brooding', 'soulful' and 'deep' (think Her, Eternal Sunshine of the Spotless Mind or High Fidelity), yet women with eccentricities are simplified as 'Manic Pixie Dream Girls'. While the MPDG is useful to call out underwritten women, Amélie has autonomy about how she lives her life, and if that is to spend her days quietly making others happy, it at least leads her to love, which she eventually finds for herself.

OTHER ROMCOMS TO BINGE:

SUBMARINE (2010)
Just as whimsical and with the same dark edge. Simply swap sunny Paris for waterlogged Wales.

GHOST WORLD (2001)
Two introverts for the price of one in this classic coming-of-age comedy about two alienated teens.

LOST IN TRANSLATION (2003)
A low-key romantic comedy heightened by its lost lovers.

WAS A LOVE LETTER TO THE 90S WOMAN

BRIDGET JONES'S DIARY

DIRECTOR: Sharon Maguire
WRITERS: Helen Fielding, Andrew Davies, Richard Curtis
YEAR: 2001

If romantic comedies are a comfort blanket, *Bridget Jones's Diary* was a 10-tog quilt. This was especially true if you were a coming-of-age millennial susceptible to the pummelling of 1990s mass-media ideals. These included being thin, white and fertile, and taking lad culture on the chin, not to mention shrugging off workplace harassment 'cos boys will be boys'!

Helen Fielding's novel *Bridget Jones's Diary* bottled the zeitgeist of the 1990s woman. Whether we liked it or not, we were given aspirations to live up to that made life feel like a game of whack-a-mole. From counting calories, to attempting recipes from *House and Garden*, women were supposed to be something between Kate Moss and Delia Smith. Then, in stumbled Bridget, with her make-up-smudged mirror, who sardonically made us realize how exhausting it all was. As she clambered through life with her accidental 'tart' outfit, a chorus of women said, 'Thank fuck, it's not just me.'

In a script that pecked at the irony of life, her pants-wearing procrastinations hit the nail on the head. While dressing for a date with her slippery boss, she remarks that tiny panties would be most attractive if the date got that far, but surely that moment will never be reached unless she wears the 'scary stomach-holding-in panties'?

Bridget would have certainly benefited from the #MeToo movement and enjoyed the body-positive era we're thankfully in. But while aspects of the film have not aged well, it serves as a last choke of air before things really got bleak. In this pre-9/11, pre-Brexit, pre-Trump, pre-social media world, women could pratfall through life without becoming a meme – yet, let's not look back with too much affection, as this is a time we refuse to go back to.

Bridget saw the romcom evolve beyond the be-all of marriage or high-school first love. Here, in the grown-up years of a woman who enjoys fags and Chardonnay, the headfuck of dating graduated to somewhere less pink. But the saving grace from seeing Bridget aspire to be a prototype is the well-earned appreciation of hearing, 'I like you just as you are.' It may have been uttered by a charming Mr Darcy, but the message is from Helen Fielding to her fellow 1990s women.

OTHER ROMCOMS TO BINGE:

CLOCKWATCHERS (1997)
A sardonic ode to women at work, battling boredom and creeps with solidarity and humor. A gem.

HAPPY GO LUCKY (2008)
A cheerful palate cleanser in the shape of Poppy, who radiates more optimism and positivity than BJ's self-deprecating doubt.

GOT US TALKING ABOUT SEXUAL FLUIDITY

KISSING JESSICA STEIN

DIRECTOR: Charles Herman-Wurmfeld
WRITERS: Heather Juergensen, Jennifer Westfeldt
YEAR: 2001

Whoever came up with the tagline 'When it comes to love, sometimes she just can't think straight' deserved to take the rest of the day off. But it's the word 'sometimes' that's now poignant in the analysis of this momentous queer film, as it was as close as 2001 mainstream romcoms got to discussing sexual fluidity.

If you've been unable to enjoy Woody Allen films since he became notoriously problematic, *Kissing Jessica Stein* provided a satisfying sub. With lemon-sharp banter across wholesome New York scenes, Jessica is our straight-laced heroine who's described as the Jewish Sandra Dee. Innocent and neurotic, she's also habitually single until she answers an ad in the paper in the women-seeking-women section. It's an ad placed by Helen, who's equally curious after failing to get her kicks with her string of casual men.

Bisexuals of the time may have felt deflated when honouring their sexual identity was curiously left unpronounced, and the fact that Jessica ends up with a man, and not Helen, is another frustration we'll chalk up to timid times. Why couldn't Jessica sometimes like men and *sometimes* like women? It's not like bisexuality hasn't always been a thing. But within this controversy of handling queer stories with conservatism, discourse on sexual fluidity was now being had. The most provocative (and

outrageous) dialogue, of course, comes from Helen's gay best friends. As one tells her she can't possibly like Jessica because she 'likes the penis', his boyfriend replies, 'Straight girl, gay girl. What's the difference? An orgasm is an orgasm.'

If the concept of bisexuality in *Kissing Jessica Stein* was apologetic, there was no identity crisis when it came to Jewish yanks. From the Shabbat dinner Jennifer's mum invites everyone and their distant cousin to, to the husband hunting on her granddaughter's behalf at a synagogue on Yom Kippur, this romcom embraced Jewish matriarchs with comical affection.

What's most heartening is Jessica's journey to acceptance, where her biggest burdens are the ones she's placed on herself. She may have been constipated with anxiety about telling people she's a lesbian, but everyone's just impressed that she's finally getting laid.

OTHER ROMCOMS TO BINGE:

CHASING AMY (1997)
Another valiant attempt to explore bisexuality, which annoyingly pussied out on using the word 'bi'.

APPROPRIATE BEHAVIOR (2015, SEE PAGE 162)
For a more unapologetic look at bisexual romcom life, this was the groundbreaker.

IMAGINE ME & YOU (2005)
Where better to realize you like women than at your own wedding to a man? A sweet, British crowd pleaser.

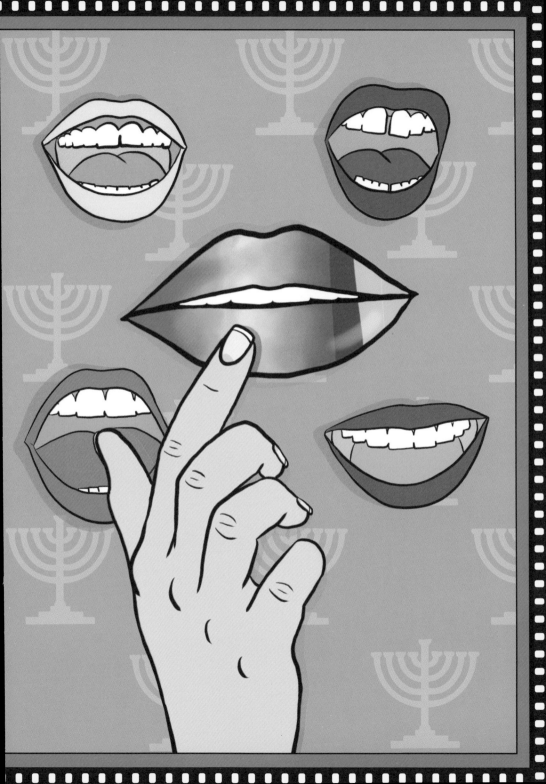

REVERSED THE 'DUMB BLONDE' STEREOTYPE

LEGALLY BLONDE

DIRECTOR: Robert Luketic
WRITERS: Amanda Brown, Karen McCullah, Kirsten Smith
YEAR: 2001

Historians claim the first recorded 'dumb blonde' was in 1775, when the play *Les Curiosités de la Foire* caricatured French courtesan Rosalie Duthé's habit of taking long pauses. This shallow depiction has since inspired famed blonde women to cunningly embrace the stereotype while challenging the judgement. In 1953 Marilyn Monroe's *Gentlemen Prefer Blondes* had a satirical underbelly (that went over many heads), but Dolly Parton's 1967 song told the world more explicitly that this 'dumb blonde ain't nobody's fool'. Then of course there's *Legally Blonde* – another cultural quake that with a $141m box office still sings Dolly's tune.

Based on the book by Amanda Brown (who mined her hostile experience of law school), Elle Woods is pretty in pink. Radiant with the expectation of her boyfriend's proposal, she's devastated when he says he needs a 'Jackie not a Marilyn' before heading to Harvard. Determined to prove she's more than her looks, she aces the entrance exam and follows him to university to win him back. Although her motivations aren't high on the feminist agenda, she learns from the journey, while teaching us the pros and persecutions of being a blonde.

Aside from hailing the power of an educated woman, *Legally Blonde* also piped up for workplace harassment. With women still being blamed for unwanted advances based on how they choose to look, it is empowering to see a woman tell her harasser where to go. Proudly hyper-feminine, Elle also ruptured the 'strong female character' emerging from the millennium, where *Miss Congeniality, Crouching Tiger, Hidden Dragon, Charlie's Angels* and *Lara Croft* were feminist dolls with a brutalist edge. But with Elle's awareness of the nourishment of women-only spaces (from the salon to the sorority house), and the use of her new smarts to defend her fellow women, she was fluffy rather than fierce, bar the 'bend and snap' flirtation technique. The best thing about Elle? She's consistently true to herself and the only thing she changes is to get herself a law degree – 'What, like it's hard?'

Who better to play Elle than golden-girl Reese Witherspoon, who went on to start her own production company, Hello Sunshine, in 2016. With a mission to produce more empowered roles for women, she's living proof of someone who's far from dumb.

OTHER ROMCOMS TO BINGE:

PLATINUM BLONDE (1931)
Blonde bombshell Jean Harlow was the early Hollywod bad girl with beauty and brains.

GENTLEMEN PREFER BLONDES (1953, SEE PAGE 28)
Where Marilyn Monroe not only owned the stereotype, but also used it to her advantage.

SHOWED HOW LIBERATING BENDING THE RULES CAN BE

BEND IT LIKE BECKHAM

DIRECTOR: Gurinder Chadha
WRITER: Gurinder Chadha,
Guljit Bindra, Paul Mayeda Berges
YEAR: 2002

When writer/director Gurinder Chadha set about making a film about a second-generation Indian girl with footballer dreams, little did she know she was about to create the highest-grossing football film ever. But Bend It Like Beckham has scored more goals than box-office success in becoming a feminist masterpiece about bending the rules and breaking free from cultural expectations.

Jesminder (Parminder Nagra) has a talent for football, which is somewhat at odds with her parents' ambitions for her making a 'full Indian meal'. To them, that's the apex of being a good woman and will lead to their desire to find her a good man. But the weight of her parents' wishes takes on a different intent when we learn of their struggles when entering racist Britain. Arriving in the UK was far from a breeze, and really, they just want her to be protected and loved.

Jess's ambitions go beyond marriage but her dreams contend with the barriers against her as a woman of colour in a masculine space. In seeing her goal she accepts the road won't be smooth, but with some little white lies she could give herself a chance. Soon her parents think she's working in a DVD shop when really she's catching the eye of football scouts in the park.

Things get trickier – and more hilarious – when she attempts to attend her sister's wedding on the day of a football trial. Of course, this leads to an explosive revelation where the family discovers – but then, crucially, understands – her deceit. As for the romance, it's not with David Beckham, whose poster on her wall is who she wants to be not be with. And as the film cues her up with football coach Joe, jetting off with her teammate (played by Keira Knightley) is the more likely affair...

At its heart, Jess's iconic happy ending is for those second-generation girls who juggle multiple identities as they switch from one cultural expectation to the next. As she wins over her family without having to cut them off, she succeeds in her mission of defining herself.

OTHER ROMCOMS TO BINGE:

ANGUS, THONGS AND PERFECT SNOGGING (2008)
Writer/director Gurinder Chadha's equally empowering romcom about a 14-year-old girl gearing up for her first snog. (That's a kiss. Not the frozen yoghurt).

BULL DURHAM (1988)
A regular feature on best sport movie lists, here Kevin Costner and Susan Sarandon score a home run on romance.

THE KISSING BOOTH (2018)
Where best friend rules were broken to follow her heart.

MADE ROOM FOR WOMEN IN A MALE-DOMINATED SPACE

BROWN SUGAR

DIRECTOR: Rick Famuyiwa
WRITERS: Michael Elliot, Rick Famuyiwa
YEAR: 2002

Hip-hop's not exactly known for its feminist values – as Erica Barry points out in *Something's Gotta Give*: 'How many words can you rhyme with "bitch"?' But *Brown Sugar's* Syd Shaw (the delectable Sanaa Lathan) would certainly interject, as this is the culture that raised her to be who she is: a powerful editor who knows the importance of writing her truth.

For years, as a reporter for famed *XXL Magazine*, Syd has started her interviews with 'When did you fall in love with hip-hop?' As answers reel off from the likes of Dr. Dre, Questlove, Common and Method Man, we are reminded of the hot-dog fest this scene really is. Syd knows exactly when she fell in love with hip-hop: 18 July 1984. It was while witnessing a rap battle where she also met Dre (Taye Diggs) and they became childhood best friends. Fast-forward 15 years, and Dre is a music exec and Syd's a journalist on the rise, but while the grind of life has kept them apart, Dre's pending marriage ignites feelings they can't ignore.

Within this 'hip-hop version of *When Harry Met Sally*' are nods to the women who triumphed over hip-hop's male supremacy. From seminal MC Queen Latifah playing best friend Francine, to pioneering DJ Angie Martinez's

cameo in their happily-ever-after scene, *Brown Sugar* is an ode to the women who made hip-hop sing. Even Syd's style is inspired by record-industry veteran Sylvia Rhone.

But it's Syd that's really the boss in this male-dominated space. Hip-hop hopefuls know she can make or break their career, and this point is further demonstrated when she loans Dre money to start his own label. Furthermore, when the first track needs that all-important radio exposure, he has to win over yet another powerful Black woman heading up the station. As the saying goes, behind every successful man, stands a woman. But in *Brown Sugar* they don't just stand there – they're calling the shots.

OTHER ROMCOMS TO BINGE:

TOP FIVE (2014)
Another film that respects a woman's place and passion for the world of hip-hop – this time starring Rosario Dawson.

POETIC JUSTICE (1993)
Like Syd, Janet Jackson's character (Justice) knows that her writing sets her free.

LOVE AND BASKETBALL (2000, SEE PAGE 94)
For another taste of how well Sanaa Lathan portrays ambition and success – this time in the male-dominated world of basketball.

KNEW SOLIDARITY WAS HOW THE WORKING CLASS SURVIVE

MAID IN MANHATTAN

DIRECTOR: Wayne Wang
WRITERS: John Hughes, Kevin Wade
YEAR: 2002

Once upon a time, *Maid in Manhattan* was due to be directed by John Hughes, with Hilary Swank as the chambermaid. As lovely as that film would have been, the movie eventually helmed by Asian-American director Wayne Wang and Puerto Rican icon Jennifer Lopez brought a new dimension to what became not just a Cinderella story but one of solidarity with women of colour.

Marisa juggles two demanding jobs – one as a single mother, the other as a maid in a posh hotel where she is told to 'strive to be invisible', but when a promotion comes up, her colleagues push her to finally be seen. While chemistry between Marisa and Republican senate hopeful Christopher hardly sparkled, the workers' sisterhood more than made up for it. They tolerate the guests' snobbery at best, indecent exposures at worst and shoulder entitled demands by uppity white women we would now call 'Karens'. While we didn't have this term in 2002, *Maid in Manhattan* created such caricatures with Caroline and Rachel who, with their disrespect for their Latin American maids (her name is Marisa – *not* Maria!), were the 'ugly sisters' in this fairytale that enjoyed outing bigots.

This rags-to-riches story was enriched by the inspired casting of Jennifer Lopez who, with her own journey from the Bronx to the Big

Time, gave audiences a taste of reality in this otherwise fantastical tale. And at a time when her behind was exoticized by the press, *Maid in Manhattan* helped her to get her own back with winking jokes about sitting on Christopher's face.

Maid in Manhattan reminds us of the importance of allies, and the systematic barriers in the way of people of colour and the working class. In a beg, borrow and steal operation, their girl from the block becomes the belle of the ball because what's a romcom without a makeover? When Marisa's cover is blown and she is momentarily sacked, her colleague Lionel quits in solidarity, telling her, 'What defines us is how well we rise after falling.' And rise she does. Marisa wins her prince, lands the promotion and we just know she'll stick to her promise when she says she'll give her colleagues a raise.

OTHER ROMCOMS TO BINGE:

SECOND ACT (2018)
Another fake it till you make it romcom that proves Hollywood can't get enough of putting Jennifer Lopez on public transport.

MARRY ME (2022)
A moment please to acknowledge that J-Lo has been the leading lady in romcoms for 20+ years.

CINDERELLA (1997)
The one with Brandy as the lead and Whitney Houston as the fairy godmother, which probably didn't mean to be as camp as it was.

KNEW THE MAKEOVER WAS FOR HER (NOT HIM)

MY BIG FAT GREEK WEDDING

DIRECTOR: Joel Zwick
WRITER: Nia Vardalos
YEAR: 2002

One of the most overused romcom tropes is the makeover montage. When bad, they suggest that if women put on a leather jacket, remove glasses and slice off the thing that makes us unique (like, say, a mermaid tail), we'll find the person of our dreams. When done right, the transformation is more than a skin-deep restyle. Just ask Toula in *My Big Fat Greek Wedding*, whose glow-up to elevate her looks as well as her brain is one of the most inspiring makeovers of all.

Fotoula 'Toula' Portokalos is the infamous lead played by writer Nia Vardalos. Sure, she's already spotted Ian in her family's Greek restaurant (where we learn he likes his potatoes spicy), but he's not the driving force behind the decision to reinvent heself. Toula wants to emancipate herself from her family's doctrine of being a nice Greek girl, with a nice Greek husband who makes nice Greek babies. Not that those things aren't important to her too, but finding herself – ahead of becoming a wife and a mother – has to come first.

Alongside the traditional montage of learning how to apply contact lenses and blusher, the biggest game changer is Toula going to college. In the poke of an eye, her new qualification lands her a job in a travel agency (not, shocker, a magazine publisher) and she soon boosts the family business with twenty-first-century tech.

Vardalos is better than allowing us to think a makeover got her the guy. Over a first date where Toula refers to her former self as 'frump girl', he says, 'I don't remember frump girl, I remember you.' Swoon. Ian does his own transformation by agreeing to be baptized in a blow-up baby pool so they can wed in their Greek Orthodox church.

Vardalos's portrayal of Greek culture saw a romcom shake-up in a swamp of white women with high metabolisms. Sticking to her guns as well as her roots, Vardalos refused film-studio suggestions to whitewash her story or sacrifice herself as lead when told she 'wasn't pretty enough to be a leading lady and not fat enough to be a character actress'. By producing the highest-grossing romcom of all time, Vardalos proved she was more than enough.

OTHER ROMCOMS TO BINGE:

CLUELESS (1995, SEE PAGE 64)
Where the makeovers 'help create a sense of control in a world of chaos'.

WORKING GIRL (1988, SEE PAGE 52)
The ultimate lesson in how power dressing cures imposter syndrome.

LAST HOLIDAY (2006, SEE PAGE 124)
Queen Latifah splurging on her makeover like there's no tomorrow? As gorgeous as it is priceless.

GOT REVENGE ON A HISTORY OF ROMCOM SEXISM

DOWN WITH LOVE

DIRECTOR: Peyton Reed
WRITERS: Eve Ahlert, Dennis Drake
YEAR: 2003

Set on the cusp of the sexual revolution, *Down with Love* is a throwback to the romcom days of yore that saw Doris Day and Rock Hudson's battle of the sexes light up late Fifties Hollywood – this time with Renée Zellweger as a bestselling author and Ewan McGregor as the man about town. With encyclopedic knowledge and loving appreciation, references to the genre's heyday are satirized with vintage zest. But the film's biggest subversion, and overlooked feminist appeal, is the comeuppance after an era of hoodwinking its female leads.

Within majors such as *It Happened One Night*, *Lover Come Back* and *The Shop Around the Corner*, a theme of deception was strengthened by box-office success. Films of the noughties still clung to this template in a way that feminist critique hadn't quite yet shut down; meanwhile, the fiercely successful *What Women Want*, *10 Things I Hate About You* and *How to Lose a Guy in 10 Days*, still profited from the plots that saw men habitually lie to women.

But *Down with Love* held the romcom to account for a history of giddy sexism that has made it hard for feminists to enjoy. With twist after twist, Barbara Novak (Zellweger) ends up fooling Catcher Block (McGregor) after her own elaborate web of lies leads to her revenge. Novak's new book – which inspires a new wave

of feminism – might be titled *Down With Love*, but she's quick to point out that this doesn't rule out sex. As now was the time to enjoy 'sex à la carte' or find pleasures in chocolate as a reasonable substitute to men.

It's not just a legacy of romcom sexism that this film ridicules. Cheekily poking fun at the no-sex sex comedies of the time (with particular affection for the exceptional *Pillow Talk*), the script is littered with so much innuendo that it begs to be spanked. In a technique that became popularized by Fifties romcoms when it helped bypass censorship of two people in bed, an inspired split screen sees our couple appear to be thrust together while saying how they'd 'love to come'.

Talking of when to come, *Down With Love* was perhaps released a bit too early as its 'flop' suggests audiences were too in love with romcoms full of lovelorn neurotic women à la Bridget Jones. But when the Covid-19 lockdown struck and comfort watching rose, many a think-piece appeared to unearth its feminist charm.

OTHER ROMCOMS TO BINGE:

SEX AND THE SINGLE GIRL (1964)
With the spirit of Barbara Novak, this single girl births a new generation of free-thinking women who treat sex 'à la carte', just like the lads.

WHILE YOU WERE SLEEPING (1995, SEE PAGE 68)
Less megalomaniac and more mushy, Sandra Bullock's character pulls off an impressive imposter act.

116

PUT A SPIN ON THE 'CRAZY' GIRLFRIEND TROPE

HOW TO LOSE A GUY IN 10 DAYS

DIRECTOR: Donald Petrie
WRITERS: Michele Alexander, Jeannie Long, Kristen Buckley, Brian Regan, Burr Steers
YEAR: 2003

To think. There was a time in the 1990s when a book called *The Rules: Time-tested Secrets for Capturing the Heart of Mr. Right* was apparently a staple for a woman's bedside table. This is according to American authors Jeannie Long and Michele Alexander, who felt compelled to write a comedy clap-back called *How to Lose a Guy in 10 Days: The Universal Don'ts of Dating.* Published in 1998, the satirical book, written hungover and on napkins, captured the shenanigans of Long and Alexander's dating history, while taking issue with a manual telling women what to do. Fast-forward five years to 2003, and Kate Hudson embodied their spirit of non-conformist women ready to challenge the rules.

In further proof that romcoms love a female journalist, here was one riffing on the absurdity of women's magazines and their habit of printing bonkers dating advice. And in a world where such mags encouraged extreme measures to nab a man – which often involved rewiring your personality or drastically changing your appearance – Kate Hudson's Andie was doing quite the reverse.

The idea that there is a right or wrong way for a woman to behave when looking for love is the crux of the comedy, which lands with genuine lols, but ultimately the assignment to sabotage a relationship in 10 days (or make someone fall in love, as McConaughey's character is on a secret bet to do) is presented as just silly, because love always finds a way. It's a message that's more delicately delivered by Andie's colleague Michelle. Although we meet her as the embodiment of the needy crazy ex-girlfriend, her behaviour can't be that bad, since her boyfriend comes crawling back.

Andie's agreement to the task of writing yet another insipid feature is completely career-driven – after all, what woman hasn't had to make sacrifices in order to get ahead? But while she's on a mission to land her big break, so she can write her dream feature on 'How to Bring Peace to Tajikistan', she simultaneously blasts the madness of giving grown women rules on how to behave. OK, her extremes are heightened for comic effect, but hey, giving someone a 'love fern' as a symbol of their affections might be someone's jam. Who are we to judge?

OTHER ROMCOMS TO BINGE:

13 GOING ON 30 (2004, SEE PAGE 122)
Rather than pandering to the institutionalized misogyny of the mag she works for, Jenna Rink rebranded it to something much less scathing.

SCOTT PILGRIM VS THE WORLD (2010)
Proof 'crazy ex boyfriends' also exist – here there are seven of them.

SAW THE 'MADE WOMAN' FOR WHO SHE REALLY IS

SOMETHING'S GOTTA GIVE

DIRECTOR: Nancy Meyers
WRITER: Nancy Meyers
YEAR: 2003

Erica Barry has it made. She's an award-winning playwright, has a beach house in The Hamptons, fearlessly wears white turtlenecks and, despite being 50-ish, is being wooed by a young hot doctor in the shape of Julian (Keanu Reeves). For someone so put together, something's gotta give.

Erica is a self-made woman who, after raising her daughter and finding peace with her divorce, is working hard to resist that distracting thing called emotion. This is put to the test when her 20-something-year-old daughter starts to date ageing chauvinist Harry (Jack Nicholson). After the initial horror comes intrigue, and after her daughter moves on to someone her own age, Harry and Erica find love.

This adorably daffy plot from the lived wisdom of romcom virtuoso Nancy Meyers still causes debate over the Julian vs Harry scenario. Admittedly, anyone who chooses Jack Nicholson over Keanu Reeves might need a nice lie-down, but it's a no-brainer when you know she's picking the man that sees her for who she really is and not just what she appears to be.

With Julian she's a famed genius playwright, which is an exhausting act to live up to; meanwhile, Harry has seen her naked in every way by managing to slice off that turtleneck. As Harry sheds the snakey skin he's slithered around in all his life, he looks as surprised as she does at their unravelling attraction, telling her, 'You are a tower of strength. I think you use your strength to separate yourself from everyone. But it's thrilling when your defences are down and you're not isolated. That, I believe, is your winning combo. Killer combo, actually.'

Erica Barry is director Nancy Meyers' gift to women who seem to have it all (or have chosen someone who looks like Jack Nicholson over Keanu Reeves). We're talking about the women whose homes are immaculate and whose careers are successful, and who are sometimes a 'highly strung, overamped, controlling, know-it-all neurotic ...' This celestial aura of greatness can either attract or intimidate, but as we begin to understand what attracts Harry and Julian to Erica ('who's also incredibly cute and lovable'), we know her decision leads her to a soulmate, not a fanboy.

OTHER ROMCOMS TO BINGE:

IT'S COMPLICATED (2009)
Another Nancy Meyers classic with a *who's she gonna pick* plot – this time with feminist demigod Meryl Streep and the less complicated decision of Alec Baldwin or Steve Martin.

THE FIRST WIVES CLUB (1996)
Why take one badass divorced woman in her fifties when you can have three, with the added bonus of Goldie Hawn and Bette Midler?

REFLECTS ON BEING
A BETTER FEMINIST

13 GOING ON 30

DIRECTOR: Gary Winick
WRITERS: Cathy Yuspa, Josh Goldsmith
YEAR: 2004

Under the fluff of this time-hop treasure, which legitimized a thirst for Mark Ruffalo and certified Jennifer Garner as a comedic boss, is the journey of a 13-year-old girl finding her feminist feet when, after unwittingly finding herself at '30, flirty and thriving', she has to suddenly deal with the fact she's been a bit of a bitch.

From stealing her friend's ideas, sleeping with a colleague's partner and punching down on her cardigan-loving colleague, future Jenna's hardly the classic ally to women. Then there's the magazine *Poise* she's now the editor of – the one that contributed to her lack of self-esteem and had her saying, 'I don't want to be beautiful in my own way, I want to look like these people.' The people she's referring to are thin, moody and dress like vanilla ice-cream, and after a lifetime of being sucked into *Poise's* aspirationally demeaning lifestyle, she's been spat into the future and landed on their payroll.

What's most disturbing on a retrospective watch is that teen Jenna looked so nice and (*whisper it*) recognizable? Who didn't pad their bra, wear too much make-up and try too hard to be liked? Jenna may be the one to have been catapulted into her thirties, but we got sucked back to our ghastly teenage years and made to question whose beauty standards we

were really living up to. And – for those who didn't look a jot like Jennifer Garner – did we ever see ourselves in mainstream media?

With her mother's wisdom about mistakes being just lessons on how to put things right, nu-age Jenna rebrands *Poise* for 'real women who are smart and pretty and happy to be who they are'. OK, she's still a lily-white teen from the suburbs and hasn't clocked intersectionality, but we'll have to have faith that she will widen that lens. Using up the last of her wishing dust, let's dream of a life for Jenna where she keeps her job after being carried over the threshold of that Calpol-coloured house, stops with the slut-shaming and uses her feminist awakening to produce the kind of magazine not just 'some women look up to', but all.

OTHER ROMCOMS TO BINGE:

MISS CONGENIALITY (2000, SEE PAGE 96)
Until she walked the catwalk in another woman's shoes, Gracie was quite the misogynist (or at least further in the closet).

BIG (1988)
Interesting how much more sexual the age-jump premise is when a boy (Tom Hanks) gets a go on the magic dust. Jenna was robbed.

BARBIE (2023, SEE PAGE 214)
Stereotypical Barbie learns that being a woman is far more complicated than she was designed to believe.

HAD A PLUS-SIZE LEAD LIVING HER BEST LIFE

LAST HOLIDAY

DIRECTOR: Wayne Wang
WRITERS: Jeffrey Price,
Peter S. Seaman, J.B. Priestley
YEAR: 2006

For those at the back who haven't been paying attention, Queen Latifah is a romcom royal. Multi-award-winning music artist aside, she has long reigned in the movie world with performances in the mighty *Brown Sugar*, *Just Wright*, *Girls Trip* and *Bringing Down the House* (which remains one of the highest-grossing romcoms ever, despite its regressive racial politics). But in *Last Holiday* she truly leads as an international lady of leisure, really living it up, and who can blame her after mistakenly being told she's got three weeks to live?

Directed by Wayne Wang (a cheerleader for the underdog - see *Maid in Manhattan*), Georgia Byrd works in a department store despite dreams of being a chef. Through her 'Book of Possibilities' (three years before Pinterest was a thing) she perfects gourmet meals for the kid next door who's basically her only next of kin. In the only hint we see towards any anxieties about her size, she won't eat them herself because she's on the Lean Cuisine diet. It's a breezy note that serves the rest of the film's theme of relishing a woman who - after a life of loneliness, coupons, poor government healthcare and wasting too much of her life 'being quiet' - is finally living out loud, free from restraint.

As she spends her life savings on travelling to The Grandhotel Pupp (a real hotel in the Czech Republic), she takes full advantage of the spa, celebrity-chef menus and opportunities to ski. And anyone holding their breath for an awkward plus-size makeover scene can relax and exhale, as the fashion boutique has just her size.

Now, Queen Latifah wasn't the first choice for this movie, but when John Candy unexpectedly passed away, the role with him in mind was soon up for grabs. In an interesting gender- and race-reversal role, the weight of Georgia's joy has all the more cushion. At a time when love for big girls scraped Hollywood's barrel, seeing Queen Latifah cuddle up to LL Cool J (whose lips deserved a supporting role Oscar) scrumptiously quenched a thirst. So, all hail Queen Latifah for consistently embracing her size. Google what she wore to this premiere and you'll see a woman comfortable in her skin with an unapologetic glow still worn today.

OTHER ROMCOMS TO BINGE:

REAL WOMEN HAVE CURVES (2002)
Anyone who says, 'My weight says to everyone, fuck you!' (as America Ferrera's character says) is a winner in this book.

PHAT GIRLZ (2006)
Mo'Nique and Kendra C. Johnson are two Pretty Hot and Thick women (yes, that abbreviates to 'Phat').

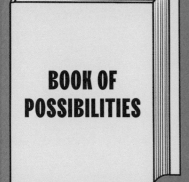

BOOK OF POSSIBILITIES

BOOK OF REALITIES

TAUGHT US ABOUT INVISIBLE LABOUR

THE BREAK-UP

DIRECTOR: Peyton Reed
WRITERS: Jay Lavender,
Jeremy Garelick, Vince Vaughn
YEAR: 2006

'What my baby wants, my baby gets,' says Gary when Brooke counts the three lemons he brought back from the store. But three lemons are not what 'baby' wants. What she wants is the kind of man who listens when she asks for 12, or at least admits he can't count. Instead, Gary (Vince Vaughn) has provided his version of what's good enough and tries to make Brooke (Jennifer Aniston) feel bad for her simple, specific request.

A Hollywood romcom that reveals the aftermath of the happily ever after and delves into the reality of how women still pick up most of the household chores, *The Break-Up* felt like a reviving slap of reality. And with the perfect casting of Jennifer Aniston, fresh from Hollywood's biggest divorce, frankly, it was just nice to see someone go through so much public heartbreak and thrive in such a cathartic role. As the world watched Brooke clutch a bag of what she didn't ask for, a chorus of women who knew only too well what it felt like to be thrown lemons sang in knowing harmony.

Of course, it's an amalgamation of all the little things that topple the tower, as *The Break-Up* so carefully observes. Neglecting to do the dishes to play video games is one thing, but having to explain that 'it will only take 15 minutes' takes up unnecessary and valuable headspace. As tension

peaks, Brooke breaks it off, prompting the rest of the movie to engage in a game of emotional chicken to see who can act like the bigger asshole. It's no spoiler that that crown goes to Gary, which is where the movie feels like a shot of solidarity for anyone whose been in a relationship where they've had to be twice the adult – as if looking after ourselves isn't hard enough.

For pinching at the topic of invisible labour, *The Break-Up* was a jolt of romcom nuance from Peyton Reed, whose *Down with Love* and *Bring It On* also flirted with feminist themes. His string of anti-romcom movies helped those born into the *American Pie* era grow up and dismantle gendered roles (even if they don't understand what a 'show lemon' is).

OTHER ROMCOMS TO BINGE:

THIS IS 40 (2012)
Another reality-check romcom of the 2010s – here we laugh and cry at the idea of keeping your shit (and family) together as you venture into your forties.

FRIENDS WITH KIDS (2011)
Across three individual couples, here's a film that shows how having a kid is like throwing a hand grenade into your relationship.

THE ONE I LOVE (2014)
An intriguing, dark comedy about a marriage in demise while trapped on a retreat at their therapist's request.

EMPOWERED WOMEN TO
PLAY THEIR OWN LEAD

THE HOLIDAY

DIRECTOR: Nancy Meyers
WRITER: Nancy Meyers
YEAR: 2006

Boyfriend cheating because you're too busy for sex? In a 'twisted toxic thing' with a married man? In these two romances for the price of one Christmas classic, Iris (Kate Winslet) and Amanda (Cameron Diaz) realize they're playing supporting characters when they thought they were the lead.

Not enough credit is given to the righteous decisions these women then make, despite being so sorely rejected. Some of us can't even get out of bed, yet Iris and Amanda pick themselves up and independently transport themselves into completely new lives in a move that should see Nancy Meyers own a share of Airbnb. Escapism has never looked so good (no, really, this is house interiors porn), and while Amanda swapped LA for a Christmas-card version of the UK in Iris's cottage, Iris is living Amanda's LA dream.

Calling *The Holiday* a cliché is a cliché in itself. In fact, it's a love letter to romantic comedy from one of the sharpest romcom writers of our time, and it delivers on its intention of being as cosy as cashmere socks. Besides, clichés are a requirement of Christmas. Nostalgia, tradition and knowing exactly what's going to happen next is comforting because nobody's got time for surprises, unless they're under a tree.

Admittedly, talking out loud is one romcom trope that verges on the ridiculous between our

gallivanting women. But isn't this just Meyers validating our internal monologue? And in a film where they are their own best friend, they've got no one else to talk to until Miles (Jack Black) and Graham (Jude Law) come along.

With its meta winks and diegetic shifts, *The Holiday* is confident in its self-awareness of paying homage to old Hollywood, where good old-fashioned romance began. Thanks to Amanda's successful career as a movie-trailer editor, as well as Iris's platonic friendship with veteran Hollywood screenwriter Arthur and her flirtations with movie-score composer Miles, the stage is set for some informed observations of how the Hollywood romance machine works.

That same machine has arguably engineered unrealistic romantic expectations and unwittingly become a factory of broken hearts. But under the messaging of *The Holiday*, we're reminded to pick ourselves up, take ourselves away and step forwards to take centre stage in our own life.

OTHER ROMCOMS TO BINGE:

PRIVATE BENJAMIN (1980)
Another Nancy Meyers classic, where Goldie Hawn stands to attention.

WHILE YOU WERE SLEEPING (1995, SEE PAGE 68)
If the man you fancy lies unconscious, what better way to woo him than to step up and play his girlfriend? How this movie isn't creepier, we'll never know.

DARED TO SUGGEST THAT NOT ALL WOMEN ARE MATERNAL

WAITRESS

DIRECTOR: Adrienne Shelly
WRITER: Adrienne Shelly
YEAR: 2007

As much as we're led to believe the opposite, a new mother's relationship with their unborn baby isn't always one of instantaneous love. That comes with a journey, and how each mother gets there is an integral quest of her own. Romcoms in 2007 discovered a fascination with this concept, as revealed in three major films that brought the genre up to date. But while *Juno* and *Knocked Up* had divisive ethics, *Waitress* was the one that explored pregnancy with the most honest clout.

We meet Jenna in the loo, clutching a stick still warm from her pee and telling her fellow waitresses, 'I don't want no baby, I just want to make pies.' Fulfilled by her creative talents, Jenna finds release in baking emotion-inspired pies. Upon a positive result, she bakes 'Bad Baby Pie', and 'I Don't Want Earl's Baby Pie' is named after the abusive husband she was planning to leave.

Jenna's relationship with her evolving foetus is both searing and blunt, as she reconciles herself with its existence outside of her womb. In one of the many letters to her bump she writes, 'I wish I could feel other things', such as love more than hindrance, at the looming prospect of parenthood. But when the baby further tethers her to her man-child of a husband, is it any wonder she feels trapped?

Jenna provides catharsis for those going through the headfuck of pregnancy and avoids any judgement for those lacking maternal instinct, because, yes, growing a human *can* feel like you've swallowed a 'parasite'. While the conservatism of the romcom in 2007 wasn't gutsy enough to bring up abortion, *Waitress* remained pro-choice when it came to what to do after birth. Within that dichotomy of exhaustion and bionic power many new mothers find, Jenna takes one look at the father and decides he's got to go – along with the charming doctor she had a rejuvenating, but ultimately whimsical, affair with. In her decision to be a single mother by choice, we see an alternative to the deemed necessity of having a man by your side. Now free to enter that pie contest, she of course wins – her daughter and new pie restaurant bring her all the love she needs.

OTHER ROMCOMS TO BINGE:

JUNO (2007)
Teenage sex! Pregnancy! Adoption!! Juno was brave for its time, but the scene at the abortion clinic still warrants debate.

KNOCKED UP (2007)
Aaannnd if you want to see an unplanned pregnancy from a man-child's point of view ...

HOME FRIES (1998)
As mad as this film is, it's buried treasure within movies about the empowerment of a pregnant woman (with said woman being Drew Barrymore).

DEMONSTRATED THE POWER OF SAYING 'NO'

27 DRESSES

DIRECTOR: Anne Fletcher
WRITER: Aline Brosh McKenna
YEAR: 2008

In a 2022 YouGov poll on people pleasing, 46 per cent of women said they felt responsible for how others feel, overshadowing 35 per cent of men. Women were also more likely than men to say they struggled to establish boundaries with others.

27 *Dresses'* Jane (Katherine Heigl) is in that people-pleasing statistic. How else would she have ended up saying yes 27 times to being a bridesmaid and attending two weddings in one night? Even her long-term job as a personal assistant (geddit?) has given her Stockholm syndrome, and she thinks she's in love with her boss George. After years of her buying him breakfast burritos and doing his laundry, George says things like, 'I can always count on you because you never say no,' which sounded creepy even in 2008. A line should have been drawn at organizing George's wedding to her sister Tess that, despite causing her all sorts of rage, has Jane smiling and nodding until she catastrophically snaps.

Besides finally learning how to say 'no', the biggest lesson from Jane's character is that - actually - she's always had the power to stick up for herself. After all, Jane did strike a very firm deal with a cabbie for a flat fare of $300 on the condition he wouldn't look in the rear-view mirror (she was changing into yet another bridesmaid dress, y'see). And this is the same woman who valiantly defended herself after Kevin - a nuptials journalist who thinks weddings 'are the last legal form of slavery' - secretly used her 27 weddings for an article and a promotion. OK, so she marries him in the end (spoiler), but he did *try* to stop it going to print after realizing it was a dick move.

One less forgiving trait of Jane's nice-girl act is the fact that she was so judgemental. Within the respectability politics of 2008, the slut-shaming of Jane's sister and her best friend (Judy Greer) is eye-rollingly accepted. But through today's modern lens we're more inclined to think that if a girl wants to use a wedding as a hunting ground, or prescribe herself some sad-girl sex in the back of a car, it's all fair enough. Isn't it great when romcoms show us how far we've come?

OTHER ROMCOMS TO BINGE:

COMING TO AMERICA (1988)
When a woman who's willing to bark like a dog is presented as Prince Akeem's queen-to-be, he literally flies to the other side of the world to find someone less ridiculous.

AMERICAN PIE (1999)
When someone as docile as Michelle finally tells us where she stuck that flute that one time in band camp, we're just really happy for her, y'know?

SANG IN THE FACE OF SLUT-SHAMING

MAMMA MIA!

DIRECTOR: Phyllida Lloyd
WRITER: Catherine Johnson
YEAR: 2008

Come for the ABBA songs, take leave from the patriarchy as my, my, *Mamma Mia!* is a feminist utopia. Within this matriarchal musical, which sees its women footloose and headstrong, Sophie, her mother Donna and their squad of female friends invite us to an island where choice is queen and sex-shaming is lost at sea.

Of course, there's plenty to gloss over. In *Mamma Mia!*, it's not the off-key singing (let's just imagine it's a celebration of imperfection) but the fact that Sophie's been reading her mum's diary. Here, she discovers her mother's sexual escapades from a time when she was enjoying the sexual liberation of the 1960s but might not have trusted that new thing called the pill. In discovering the identities of the three men that could be her father, she invites them all to her wedding, in the hope one could walk her down the aisle.

Reading about your mother's sex life is a little odd but rather than cringing, Sophie sings her mum's praises and later tells her she doesn't care if she slept with 'hundreds of men'. Donna's friends are also delighted by their friend's former sex life, and when she says she was a 'stupid, reckless little slut' who had to 'grow up', thrice-married Tanya shoos away her shame and tells her to 'grow back down'.

In a film where the women spend a lot of time pushing men to the side to lyrically unite, *Mamma Mia!* has many feminist threads. By reclaiming the song 'Does Your Mother Know' – an ABBA tune that originally tuts at the advances a young girl makes to an older man – we see the power move of an older woman keeping a young man at bay. And after her parents disowned her for getting pregnant, Donna leaves the country, opens a hotel as a single mother and wakes up every morning to thank Christ she hasn't got 'some middle-aged, menopausal man' to bother her.

As for Sophie, this whole song and dance makes her re-evaluate family ideals and the traditions of marriage. Despite deciding all three are worthy of being her dad, why should any of them give her away when it's her mother who made her who she is? Thanks to learning more about her mother's life, she sees that she too has a lot of life to live and perhaps getting married to Sky is no longer the limit.

OTHER ROMCOMS TO BINGE:

MOONSTRUCK (1987, SEE PAGE 46)
Affairs are complicated and judgement should be reserved, as beautifully examined in this Cher-led classic.

I'M NO ANGEL (1933, SEE PAGE 18)
Where Mae West literally has bros in different area codes.

WHAT'S YOUR NUMBER? (2011)
Anna Faris riffs on the judgement surrounding how many people a woman has slept with.

EXPLORED ALL OPTIONS WHEN IT CAME TO HAVING KIDS

SEX AND THE CITY

DIRECTOR: Michael Patrick King
WRITERS: Michael Patrick King,
Candace Bushnell, Darren Star
YEAR: 2008

With its loyal inbuilt TV audience desperate to see Miranda, Samantha, Carrie and Charlotte graduate to the big screen, it's no wonder *Sex and the City* is one of the highest-grossing romantic comedies to date. Of course, crushing the essence of a six-season series into one (overlong) film would struggle with expectation, but with its 50 per cent Rotten Tomatoes critic score, it could have been worse.

Critic percentages aside, there's no denying the cultural impact the *Sex and the City* brand has wrought. In revolutionizing the power of female friendships, luxuriating in the spending power of affluent career women and surpassing the boundaries for sex on TV, the pleasures of women (albeit rich and white ones) were brash, beautiful and aspirationally at the fore. But while these topics are what we've come to associate with *SATC*, their maternal representations deserve a further nod of respect.

Choice is explored, depicting judgement-free decisions over the use of one's womb: there's the triumphantly objectionable Samantha (who famously threw an 'I don't have a baby shower' party), Charlotte's conception struggles and her joys of adoption, and then there's Miranda becoming pregnant after a one-night stand. But it's Carrie's muted nonchalance that's perhaps

the most powerful, as the only babies she's making are the books she writes. Sometimes the most positive representation is not to entertain the conversation at all.

The topic remains untouched when her partner Big buys them a home, with no mention of making room for a ridiculously expensive cot. Even the kitchen is dismissed as a bit unnecessary when Carrie admits she'd only use the stove as a closet. OK, so this theory does unravel by the time we get to that awkward sequel where Carrie wonders if life with 'just' Big will be big enough, but with *Sex and the City 2's* 15 per cent Rotten Tomatoes critic score, let's just agree that that movie doesn't really exist.

Along with the therapeutic virtues of brunch with your mates, our leads embrace today's liberties with what women do with our ovaries. And whether we're aggressively against kids or quietly for, talking out loud to friends and dismissing societal expectations is the healthiest way to make those decisions for ourselves.

OTHER ROMCOMS TO BINGE:

WHAT TO EXPECT WHEN YOU'RE EXPECTING (2012)
Does little for gender norms when it comes to men vs women in parenting, but is just about funny enough to be given a pass.

AWAY WE GO (2009)
Maya Rudolph in a warm, honest and insightful romantic dramedy on the big decisions couples make about bringing a little one into the world.

WAS THE REVENGE OF THE '**PERFECT QUIRKY GIRLFRIEND**'

500 DAYS OF SUMMER

DIRECTOR: Marc Webb
WRITERS: Scott Neustadter, Michael H. Weber
YEAR: 2009

After a crop of quirky underwritten women popped up like daisies in romcoms (particularly those written by men), *500 Days of Summer* presented a sliver of revenge. While many labelled Summer (Zooey Deschanel) as the poster girl for the negative cliché of the 'Manic Pixie Dream Girl', some keenly recognized that she was turning it on its pretty little head.

In this anti-romcom, Tom (Joseph Gordon-Levitt) is having a sad boy summer after being dumped by the girl he thought was The One. As he recalls the last 500 days, we see how Summer's love existed in his entitled imagination and he conveniently ignored her when she said, 'I'm not looking for anything serious.'

Through Tom's puppy-dog eyes, we see how Summer shares his taste in British rock, and that she makes him feel – in a truly endearing dance number – like he's starring in a music video to Hall & Oates' 'You Make My Dreams'. What we do know for certain about Summer is how good she is at setting boundaries after being consistently clear that she 'doesn't feel comfortable being anyone's anything'.

Tom is a warning for anyone buying into the idea that the perfect girl exists, a girl who teaches 'soulful young men to embrace life and its infinite mysteries and adventures', as described by film critic Nathan Rabin, who coined the 'Manic Pixie Dream Girl' trope. It's an observation he now laments due to its misogynistic misuse, as being 'quirky' doesn't pigeonhole women – roles written to prop up a male fantasy do.

In the wholesome stock of boy meets girl, romcoms with male leads can present an ideology of finding the dream girl who completes them. What lesser films failed to explore was what a nightmare that would be, as being responsible for someone else's happiness isn't romantic, it's a burden. That tide began to turn thanks to *500 Days of Summer*, which held up a wry mirror to how ridiculous idolization is. And as Summer called it off, she took one for the team for women who had been put so far up on a pedestal that they needed a ladder to get down.

OTHER ROMCOMS TO BINGE:

THERE'S SOMETHING ABOUT MARY (1998)
There *is* something about Mary: she's being stalked.

ETERNAL SUNSHINE OF THE SPOTLESS MIND (2004)
'Too many guys think I'm a concept, or I complete them, or I'm gonna make them alive.' Kate Winslet also clapped back at the idea of being perfect.

RUBY SPARKS (2012)
The perils of not just fantasizing about a woman, but also writing her into a warped reality. Team Ruby all the way.

CRITIQUED BACKWARDS ATTITUDES TO SEXUALITY

EASY A

DIRECTOR: Will Gluck
WRITER: Bert V. Royal
YEAR: 2010

Romcoms love riffing off old literature classics. Whether it's Jane Austen providing the backdrop for *Bridget Jones's Diary* or *10 Things I Hate About You* harking back to Shakespeare, the best teen romantic comedies were once written with quills. But rarely has a romantic comedy aligned itself so evidently as *Easy A*'s remix of Nathaniel Hawthorne's *The Scarlet Letter*. In this 1850s story about an adulterous woman, we're reminded that misogynistic labels are as old as time, but with *Easy A*'s squeeze of Gen Z zest, the tables attempt a turn for a more empowering tale.

In this 2010 Emma Stone-catapulting classic, *Easy A* tackles how sexual reputations are less forgiving for a girl. It's something our heroine Olive is learning the hard way when her white lie about losing her virginity brands her a 'whore'. It's a shame that lying about the fact you've lost your virginity is safer than admitting you spent the weekend painting your dog's nails, but this is the hellfire of high school, and you simply cannot win. Inspired by the slut-shaming 'A' emblem that Hawthorne's Hester Prynne is forced to don, Olive uses her English class text in a can't-beat-them-join-them ploy. Soon she's strutting down corridors in an A-embellished corset, pretending to live up to the brand she's

been forced to embody.

Olive shows the power of owning one's label and the satisfaction one can have for a good clap back, and it's canny to see her use the shaming to her advantage when outcasts and closet gays pay her to boost their rep. This short-lived fist pump soon slips into reality when it outs the hypocrisy of double standards between girls, guys and gays. And as outcast dudes rack up their cool points, Olive has to physically push away the boys who are now taking her for granted.

Perhaps if 1800s Hester had had access to the internet, 'humble silence' (two concepts Olive states she is 'not comfortable with') would not have been her way to deal with the public wrath. Instead, we see Olive using the relatively new and liberating tools of her generation to live-stream her truth and shut everybody up.

OTHER ROMCOMS TO BINGE:

YES, GOD, YES (2019)
Progressive for making young women feel normal about their sexual desires.

AUSTENLAND (2013)
A Jane Austen theme park to find your perfect man sounds so bad it's good.

THE TO DO LIST (2013, SEE PAGE 154)
Aubrey Plaza's sexual bucket list comes with no shame attached.

POINTED OUT THAT LOVE WASN'T ENOUGH

GOING THE DISTANCE

DIRECTOR: Nanette Burstein
WRITERS: Geoff LaTulippe
YEAR: 2010

Maybe Disney planted the idea that love conquers all, giving a pass to some curiously creepy behaviour from a parade of princes. Perhaps it was Shakespeare – the supremo romcom connoisseur – but his stories didn't exactly all end well. Wherever this idea came from, it's time to be real because, as much as the basic romcom leads us to believe that love is all you need, for a woman in a crumbling economic climate, you've gotta support yourself first.

Going the Distance brings that message home, as we see a sobering approach to practical love. Directed by former documentarian Nanette Burstein, with an R-rated bag of realism along for the ride, we meet Garrett and Erin (Justin Long and Drew Barrymore), in equally decaying professions. He's signing bands and she's trying to write for print within the digital boom that saw many of its practitioners redundant.

With more airport scenes than the average romcom, our lovers decide that after a whirlwind romance in NYC, they're prepared to go long-distance when she goes back to San Fran. But when loneliness (and horniness) begins to chafe, they decide she should join him and live on the East Coast. Thing is, there are no jobs for Erin in New York (and the mag she interned with has just gone bust) and her move means turning down her dream job on a magazine at home. While she may be moving in with the current love of her life, at 31 she'd have go back to waiting tables and living on his wage.

A more lovesick romcom would have rolled credits after Erin forgoes ambition for love. Yet, in a gratifying twist, her dream job opportunity sees her take flight. And with some warming compassion for our determined lead, Erin isn't doomed to a life of loneliness because she chose her career ...

Going the Distance takes a welcome responsible tack, in a film that encourages women to nurture their careers. Of course, it's nice to cuddle up with someone at the end of the day, but if your security and sanity rely on another person's unpredictable income, it's hardly the liberation of independence our foremothers fought for.

OTHER ROMCOMS TO BINGE:

NIGHTS AND WEEKENDS (2008)
More long-distance love high jinks, with a mumblecore twist that started Greta Gerwig's rise.

THE NOTEBOOK (2004)
Although the only time this searing romance has ever been 'funny' is when it's mentioned in *Going the Distance* as an ironic post-break-up watch.

PROVED, ONCE AGAIN, THAT WOMEN ARE FUNNY

BRIDESMAIDS

DIRECTOR: Paul Feig
WRITERS: Kristen Wiig, Annie Mumolo
YEAR: 2011

Every so often the myth that women aren't funny rears its ugly head. It's a weary charge that, despite being routinely quashed, puts women-driven comedy back to that exhausting place of having to prove itself all over again. It's as if Whoopi Goldberg, Lucille Ball, Goldie Hawn, and all those spectacularly sassy women of Hollywood's golden age never existed.

After the prodigious success of 2009's *The Hangover*, Hollywood was so dazzled by the dude-centric caper, it conveniently forgot that funny women could be profitable unless they were fart free and adorably quirky – after all, 2009 was the year of smash hit *500 Days of Summer* that shot Zooey Deschanel to fame. But then came *Bridesmaids*. A film that married gross-out humour with a 'chick flick' and went on to be coined by the *Guardian*'s Zoe Williams as 'more feminist than *Thelma and Louise*'. *Bridesmaids'* $306m box office aside, liberated female comedians, giving them access to the kind of toilet humour expected of men, and by placing grotesque comedy within the typically feminine space of a wedding, funny women no longer had to sever their femininity in order to get laughs.

Director Paul Feig talks of the pressure he felt to ensure *Bridesmaids's* success. Many of his female-writer friends were sitting on comedic women-led scripts, but were told they had to 'wait and see how *Bridesmaids* does' before getting the green light. They needn't have worried. Thanks to Maya Rudolph, Kristen Wiig, Rose Byrne, Rebel Wilson and Melissa McCarthy (all in varying degrees of shapes, sizes and ability to hold in their diarrhoea) the film went on to be coined '*The Hangover* for women' and earned a rare R-rating, which only added to the intrigue.

Bridesmaids received two Oscar nominations from an award body who aren't known for favouring either women or laughs. But another win was its depiction of wholesome female friendships and clapping back at movies such as *Bride Wars*, which enjoyed seeing manicured women with their claws out. And with the approval of audiences and awards bodies alike, Hollywood was ready to accept a new wave of funny women that saw *Trainwreck*, *Girls Trip* and *Booksmart* follow in its wake.

OTHER ROMCOMS TO BINGE:

THE SWEETEST THING (2002)
Beat *Bridesmaids* to the punch in its celebration of gross-out women (minus the critical acclaim).

BACHELORETTE (2012)
This chaotic R-rated caper saw a pre-wedding party get way, way out of hand.

BLOCKERS (2018)
Three girls. One mission: to lose their virginity on the biggest day yet (prom night).

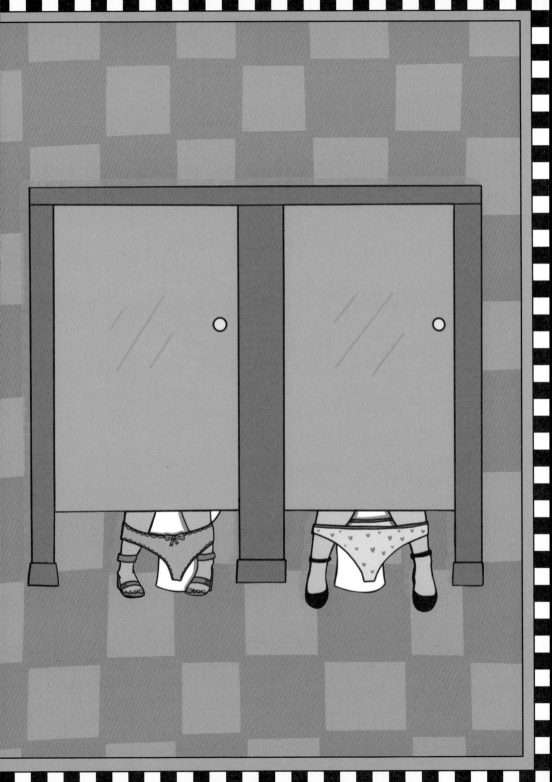

NORMALIZED THE FACT THAT WOMEN HAVE SEX BUDDIES

FRIENDS WITH BENEFITS

DIRECTOR: Will Gluck
WRITERS: Keith Merryman,
David A. Newman, Will Gluck
YEAR: 2011

Anyone who knows what the Swinging Sixties were famous for knows non-committal sex is nothing new. But after the AIDS pandemic of the 1980s, internet-driven misogyny of the 1990s and almost a decade of Republican Bush, the heydays of non-judgemental bed hopping seemed but a hippy dream. Yet from 2010, female-targeted films with a fuck-buddy premise seemed to be on the rise. Was the hesitant world of Hollywood ready to accept 'FWBs' as a thing and agree that actually they worked out quite well for women?

While *No Strings Attached* and *Love & Other Drugs* both attempted to be liberal in their portrayals of a woman's sexual freedom, *Friends with Benefits* made the biggest impression, with the most favourable critical reviews. It also didn't hurt that in the kind of casting that should have won a Pulitzer Prize, the blazing chemistry of Justin Timberlake (Dylan) and Mila Kunis (Jamie) saw two of the hottest, coolest kids on the block properly get it on in a romcom that was more lewd than prude.

Despite some iffy rationalizations into why someone could possibly want to engage in such willy-nilly sex, *Friends with Benefits* offered a positive demonstration of a woman explicitly expressing both her sexual needs and emotional boundaries. While feelings inevitably develop later on, Jamie's 'No relationships. No emotions. Just sex' rule sees her lay down the law before they lie down. As a result, the sexual escapades look genuinely fun and are always tit for tat. They both get as naked as each other, they both verbally approve of being able to 'work with' what they see, and are consistently communicative about what they do and don't like in bed, because isn't sex best when you're both on the same page?

In a modern arrangement that sits somewhere between humping a total stranger and saving your V plate until marriage, having a friend you trust enough to fornicate with gives a whole new meaning to the idea of safe sex.

OTHER ROMCOMS TO BINGE:

NO STRINGS ATTACHED (2011)
Two films with exactly the same premise released mere months apart? Hollywood really approved of us shagging our mates.

DATING AND NEW YORK (2021)
Friends with benefits for the Instagram generation, which sees him fall first to her non-committal charms.

UP IN THE AIR (2009)
Alex makes it abundantly clear why she's having sex with a character played by George Clooney. Hint, it's not marriage ... She's already got one of those.

SAW HER TRIUMPH FROM MISOGYNISTIC LABELS

SILVER LININGS PLAYBOOK

DIRECTOR: David O. Russell
WRITERS: David O. Russell, Matthew Quick
YEAR: 2012

By 2012, in an effort to try to distance themselves from such a passé genre, romcoms evolved by hiding behind 'edge'. *Silver Linings Playbook*'s 'edge' was that of mental health. Although many considered this the breakthrough of the film, the feminist value lies in the affront of a woman who's exhausted by labels and the hypocrisy of men.

In this boy-meets-girl-meets-breakdown masterpiece, which scored five Oscar nominations and a win for Jennifer Lawrence's Tiffany, Pat (Bradley Cooper) is fresh from being sectioned, after a violent reaction to his wife's infidelity highlighted undiagnosed bipolar.

Curiously undiagnosed beyond being a bit depressed, Tiffany is trying to fuck her way to sanity after her husband passed away. Diverting gloom within the mind with pleasure of the body isn't a new fix, but here Tiffany's branded a 'slut', given a cocktail of meds or asked to divulge her encounters to the titillation of Pat. When Pat's therapist questions his bitching, asking, 'Why is she a slut?' such labelling at least gets a necessary probe; 'Maybe she just needs a friend,' he suggests, allowing his professionalism to deflect judgement while knowing too well this behaviour is acceptable for men.

What's rich is that Tiffany is actually the sanest in a cast of characters who would all benefit from a therapist's couch. With her candid truths, honest self-reflection and rejection of the theory that women are either mother or whore, her lines toast tired women everywhere with a cup of recognition. In a tirade against Pat she bellows, 'I was a big slut, but I'm not anymore. There's always gonna be a part of me that's sloppy and dirty, but I like that, with all the other parts of myself. Can you say the same about yourself, fucker?!' Using that same fire, she later snaps, 'I do all this shit for other people and then I wake up and I'm empty, I have nothing!' Preach.

Truth is, Tiffany's neither a 'slut' nor a bad omen (as Pat's dad claims when his sports team starts to lose), and once everyone accepts she's just more courageous than crazy, we end on the message that truth and love can be the cure.

OTHER ROMCOMS TO BINGE:

THE APARTMENT (1960)
Another classic romcom with a mental health edge, also lauded with Oscars ('cause the Academy love grit).

EASY A (2010, SEE PAGE 140)
A masterclass in owning your 'slut' label.

WHAT'S YOUR NUMBER? (2011)
The one where Anna Faris riffs on the double standard of how many people a woman has slept with.

CENTRED THE BLACK BUTCH LESBIAN

STUD LIFE

DIRECTOR: Campbell X
WRITER: Campbell X
YEAR: 2012

With scrappy charm and a cool, shrewd wit, Campbell X heeded the rallying call of *The Watermelon Woman* (where fellow film-maker Cheryl Dunye questioned the dearth of Black lesbian stories) and helped fill the void with the unapologetic *Stud Life*. With Dunye's same fourth-wall-breaking zeal, X's handsome lead JJ talks to us directly on her YouTube show *Just Sayin*. Between these intimate interactions, and her dating escapades with gay best friend Seb, a world was unleashed that set the Black butch lesbian free.

Far from a traditional romcom where we are spoon-fed to a happily ever after, from beginning to end we're kept on our toes. JJ wakes up next to Seb but we soon understand their love is platonic, as they jokingly shriek about his erect morning wood. Smooth, suave JJ, and pretty punk Seb make quite the Batman and Robin of gay nightclubs and bars. As she straps down her breasts and he chops up cocaine with pink nail-varnished hands, they take into the night to woo and be wooed. When JJ spies Elle - a sultry 'back a yard' femme - Elle's equally intrigued and a hot romance ensues.

As the tale unfolds over Seb and JJ's beefy love stories (and the ones we encounter within their day job as photographers at gay weddings), we witness the antics of dating while

queer. From ducking have-a-go lesbians in the loo to dodging violent homophobia on the street, *Stud Life* doesn't hold back on the realities of their life. And when we see Elle and JJ deliberate how they'll first make love, JJ croons, 'The truth is there ain't no thing as real lesbian sex. It takes all sorts to make the lesbian nation.'

As *The Watermelon Woman* used terms of endearment about the lesbian community, such as 'bulldaggers' and 'sapphic sisters', JJ too casually shuffles through a lexicon of terms to describe her people. 'Stone butch', 'studs' and 'boner dykes' all pepper the script, spearheading the breadth and depth of identities within a lesbian sphere. In addition to this worldbuilding of Black British life, casual use of Jamaican patois is spoken over bashment in clubs. For those in the Black butch London club scene, X had your back in making you feel heard, seen and loved.

OTHER ROMCOMS TO BINGE:

THE WATERMELON WOMAN (1996, SEE PAGE 72)
The original Black female romcom with that same boyish charm.

BUTCH JAMIE (2007)
The one that centred the white butch lesbian.

BROS (2022)
It may not centre one Black butch lesbian (because there simply are not enough yet), but for its spectrum of representation across its all-queer cast, *Bros* was a breakthrough even in 2022.

PROVED FEMALE FRIENDSHIP IS WHERE REAL LOVE LIES

FRANCES HA

DIRECTOR: Noah Baumbach
WRITERS: Greta Gerwig, Noah Baumbach
YEAR: 2012

Before Frances Ha, there were Sophie and Frances: two 27-year-old girls who shared a roof, a bed and a language of their own. While Frances has a boyfriend, her loyalties are with her girlfriend, as the fun they have together eclipses all else. For this brief moment in time, they dream of a future life of 'lovers and no children', wisely advise that 'ahoy there' is not a good booty-call opener and lull each other to sleep with the bedtime 'story of us'.

In one of the most searing romantic comedies on female friendships, Frances Ha bottles this feeling for anyone whose most significant relationship has been with their best friend. While we are introduced to Sophie and Frances as inseparable, we soon see them float apart with the rising tide of life and new love. As we see Frances more out of sync than ever in her usual attempts to be a dancer, we're reminded that female friendships are bona fide romances that make us feel just as tripped up when they mysteriously end. And when we try to fill the void with new lovers or friends, the gap they can't fill only worsens the wound.

Female friendships have long been afforded a deeper level of connection than male friendships, perhaps due to unfair macho attitudes on how men should behave around each other. While romcoms such as I Love You, Man and That Awkward Moment have helped loosen frigid male companionships, women can freely admit when our girlfriends are our world.

Yet, in a rare depiction of such platonic intimacy, Frances Ha laments how such affections rarely last. But at least these relationships help to identify what we want from our life partners when they set a high bar for how to enjoy life. When Frances flops around her post-Sophie universe, she drunkenly delivers more wisdom than the average sober psychologist. Drawing on that 'secret world that exists in public' that she once shared with Sophie, she knows she has already set a standard for identifying her 'person in this life'.

OTHER ROMCOMS TO BINGE:

THE WORST PERSON IN THE WORLD (2021)
Spoiler, she's not. She's actually very relatable to anyone stumbling through love and life.

BOOKSMART (2019)
For more adorable friendship vibes that feel all the more intense when you're young.

ROMY AND MICHELE'S HIGH SCHOOL REUNION (1997)
Two women who, even after all these years, only want to hang out with each other.

PUT THE EMPHASIS ON HER ORGASM OVER HIS

THE TO DO LIST

DIRECTOR: Maggie Carey
WRITERS: Maggie Carey
YEAR: 2013

After a torrent of films about pubescent boys losing their virginity (and the odd 40-year-old man), at last came a film from a teenage girl's point of view. And by playfully tugging on some Gloria Steinem theory, this girl proves there's nuance between 'the virgin or the whore'.

It's summer 1993 and Brandy (Aubrey Plaza) is college-bound with her cherry intact. Being an overachieving 'mathlete' has meant she's been too busy to bone, but faced with the prospect of not being good at something, she valiantly tells her vagina it's time to get schooled.

Set in a time when the Urban Dictionary was but a twinkle in the eye of the internet, and cinema releases that grappled with a woman's sexuality that year were *Indecent Proposal* and *Boxing Helena* (*shudder*), Brandy relies on the honesty of her female friends and her family to provide an authentic explanation of how sex really goes down. Her 20-strong list goes from handjobs to rim jobs – 'so many jobs!' – and as she works her way up to orgasmic-inducing sex, the guys she works with discover her sexual pilgrimage and are in awe – not disgust – of 'such a mature quest'. The only reservation comes from her father, who reflects the hypocrisy over how society treats its girls: sexualizing them is a bit of harmless fun, but the buck stops there if that girl is ever their daughter.

What *The To Do List* ticks off with casual ease is presenting that bleary bubble of time when teenagers play with each other's genitals (not to mention their own). And why should that be limited to just boys, when girls too have sexual urges? And, yes, there are so many ways to explore consensual sexual gratification, but although sex is significant, it ain't always that deep.

Her frivolous antics do, however, have consequences, in a pointed gender-flipped plot that sees one guy fall in love. Yet, this film is more coolly about female friendship and how, in the grand scheme of life, you're more likely to remember the girls you sang Bette Midler songs with than some cherry-picking dude who came too soon.

OTHER ROMCOMS TO BINGE:

TURN ME ON, DAMMIT! (2011)
Frank, funny and feminist, this wry Norwegian romcom deals with raging teen-girl hormones.

YES, GOD, YES (2019)
Unsaintly thoughts take over a Catholic schoolgirl in this honest, smart and affectionate romcom.

BANANA SPLIT (2018)
Watch this Gen Z romcom written by a Gen Z girl for a ripe and refreshing film with authenticity and heart.

154

MADE MIDDLE-AGED DATING LOOK YOUNG AT HEART

ENOUGH SAID

DIRECTOR: Nicole Holofcener
WRITER: Nicole Holofcener
YEAR: 2013

Romantic comedies aren't just for the young and restless, as this middle-aged masterpiece so brilliantly contests. Here, in the hands of writer/director Nicole Holofcener (think a bohemian Nancy Meyers of independent film), we have vibrant divorcees blooming in their autumnal years.

Our second-time-around lovers are Eva (Julia Louis-Dreyfus) and Albert (James Gandolfini), who connect after a party and discover they're in the same boat: their only daughters are about to leave for college, which brings up all sorts of feelings about being that bit more alone. They may be fully grown but they have banter for days and their sophisticated flirting is full of juvenile glee. And while a sillier film would see their kids as a dating barrier, Eva's and Albert's children respect the fact that Mum and Dad are getting laid. Seeing parents – especially mothers – as actual people is also this film's strength, as too many romcoms paint them as shrill and overprotective, or cheerfully baking a pie. Instead, the relationship they have with their daughters is one of love and respect, and only the odd strop.

With a realistic representation of post-divorce courting, *Enough Said* reassured those marginalized by Hollywood (40+ women and plus-size men) that they needn't die alone. Also, when revising the dated battle of the sexes

theme with more worldly insight, we realize it's not gender that causes friction, but being with someone you've outgrown. Leaning into the benefits of age, it's a wisdom only the middle-aged can confidently share – after all, it tends to take having kids and a mortgage to see if a relationship can truly survive. As we meet Eva's and Albert's exes (in some significant curveball antics), we see adults making their own mind up about matters of the heart. Eva *could* allow herself to be influenced by Albert's ex-wife's quibbles or she could know she's old enough to decide for herself.

Eva's friend makes a convincing case for getting back on the love wagon: 'Maybe second marriages work because people have figured out how to compromise.' Meanwhile, James Gandolfini represents someone who deserved a second look and shouldn't be taken for granted. Despite embodying the shrine of TV's most lauded gangster in *The Sopranos*, this superb change of lane reminds us of how versatile people can be.

OTHER ROMCOMS TO BINGE:

LAST CHANCE HARVEY (2008)
Dustin Hoffman and Emma Thompson do the love, laughs and last chances thing with style.

AT MIDDLETON (2013)
That feeling when you realize your kid's college tour is great for picking up divorcees. A handsome, modest romcom for the middle aged and middle class.

156

HAD HONEST CONVERSATIONS ABOUT TRANS SEX

BOY MEETS GIRL

DIRECTOR: Eric Schaeffer
WRITER: Eric Schaeffer
YEAR: 2014

After a death march of films that portrayed trans lives as anything but light, *Boy Meets Girl* was a welcome warm breeze. Candid and forthright, yet as sweet as can be, this 2014 indie gem handled questions about trans bodies and sex with a coy brazen charm.

Reimagining the boy-meets-girl mechanics of a heteronormative plot, 20-something Ricky tells her childhood friend Robby she's looking for matrimonial love (no prizes for where that one goes). 'I haven't even found one good guy who doesn't wanna just get in my pants. Maybe I should date girls. How bad could it be?' Cue the virginal Francesca, who takes quite a shine to Ricky despite an engagement ring from a brooding marine weighing her down.

Confident, yet humble, ambitious while down to earth, Ricky's dialled-down modesty provides a trans woman with chill. The love triangles of the plot provoke illuminating conversations: Robby bumbles through explanations of how to make love to a 'va-jay-jay' for the benefit of Ricky's curiosity, and when she and Francecsa plot to consummate their attraction, they discuss how Fran can't get pregnant – no, nothing comes out anymore, and yes, it still feels good.

While much of this sounds like a stiff sex-education class, its free-flowing humour provides revelation and light. But it's by gracefully

revealing Ricky's bare moonlit body that *Boy Meets Girl* confronts the erasure of trans bodies on screen. As Ricky elegantly rises from a dip in a lake, she asks, 'You still think I'm beautiful?' to someone who wholeheartedly agrees.

While we know cinema lacks a grounded representation for anyone who isn't cisgendered, straight, non-disabled and white, at least independent film has more freedom to express reality – and in an additional pump of ethical representation, Ricky is played by trans woman Michelle Hendley. When Ricky tells Robby, 'You thank God for *Glee* every day or you'd still think scissoring was a mixed martial arts tap-out hold,' we can chuckle at the informative power that pop culture can hold. And by affording a trans girl the liberty to navigate her version of coming of age, we can thank the perfect vehicle of the romcom to crack in some loving light.

OTHER ROMCOMS TO BINGE:

ANYTHING'S POSSIBLE (2022, SEE PAGE 206)
A sweet, contemporary and honest portrayal of trans love and life that ends on a high.

DIFFERENT FOR GIRLS (1996)
Wrapped in 90s British charm, this gutsy, clumsy romcom gets a gold star for effort.

ELVIS & MADONNA (2010)
Kitsch, colorful and frilly around the edges, this cute Brazilian romcom centers a trans woman hairdresser and her tomboy lesbian lover.

HAD ZERO-JUDGEMENT ABOUT ABORTION

OBVIOUS CHILD

DIRECTOR: Gillian Robespierre
WRITERS: Gillian Robespierre, Karen Maine, Elisabeth Holm
YEAR: 2014

Obvious Child did what *Dirty Dancing* did for the romantic drama and made up for what *Knocked Up* didn't dare touch – to portray abortion with zero judgement. While *Knocked Up* also sees its leads get pregnant after a drunken night out, *Obvious Child* positions abortion as a perfectly reasonable option for a middle-class woman in 2014's New York.

Aside from positively representing choice over what women do with their ovaries, *Obvious Child* sets its sights on both loving the romcom and dismantling its clichés. Here the best friend with the best lines has stepped into the limelight, giving us Donna – a lead who's a stand-up comedian played by hilarious *Saturday Night Live* star Jenny Slate. In picking up from where *Bridesmaids* and *The Sweetest Thing* left off about bodily fluids, Donna also feels empowered enough to joke about vaginal discharge and the things she could do with her 'butt hole'.

Although such liberties are still having to be defended, *Obvious Child* recalls a time when abortions were more complicated during a tender moment that sees Donna's mother talk of her own abortion in the time before Roe vs Wade, in the 1960s. And when her best friend Nellie discusses her own abortion story, she is both pragmatic about having no regrets and

poignantly articulate over the political hypocrisy of 'living in a patriarchal society where a group of weird old white men in robes get to legislate our c****.'

Seeing *Obvious Child*'s leading women discuss their abortion experience is reflective of a world where they are common, despite Hollywood trying to pretend they don't exist or are something to regret. *Knocked Up* couldn't even bring itself to utter the word abortion ('schma-shmortion' doesn't count), and *Juno* saw a pregnant 16-year-old bolt from the clinic after walking past a one-person anti-abortion vigil.

Obvious Child does its romcom service by proving that romance, and female solidarity, can live anywhere – even in the waiting room of an abortion clinic on Valentine's Day. This is where Donna and Max's open-ended happily ever after lies, but it's also where Donna acknowledges the other women in the waiting room. As they share a warm smile of solidarity, they are united for that moment by their freedom of choice.

OTHER ROMCOMS TO BINGE:

UNPREGNANT (2020)
Exhibit A of how unwanted pregnancies and road-trip movies go hand in hand when having to drive across America to find a legal abortion.

GRANDMA (2015)
Exhibit B, with Lily Tomlin at the wheel as the badass Grandma of dreams.

WAS UNAPOLOGETICALLY BISEXUAL

APPROPRIATE BEHAVIOR

DIRECTOR: Desiree Akhavan
WRITER: Desiree Akhavan
YEAR: 2015

While we may be beginning to enjoy more fluid conversations about the spectrums of sexuality, in 2015 things were still a little stale. Bisexuality, in particular, was still something of a novelty and pop culture wasn't doing much to help. From the otherwise sexually fluent Carrie Bradshaw calling it a 'layover to Gaytown' to Phoebe from *Friends* singing that bisexuals were 'kidding themselves', it seemed that such an identity was too ambiguous a concept for the mainstream to grasp. Thankfully, *Appropriate Behavior* became a bisexual breakthrough that did its bit to put people, ahem, straight.

Off screen and on, Desiree Akhavan wears many hats. While writing and directing *Appropriate Behavior*, she also stars as Shirin – an art-imitating-life bisexual Iranian-American failing to live up to expectations. From appeasing her well-heeled Persian family, who are ignoring the fact she's 'a little bit gay', to being politically correct with her butch ex-girlfriend Maxine, who doesn't take kindly to being called a 'dyke', Shirin is a lost Brooklynite ship searching for a hipster shore.

Shirin's raw break-up gives her time to reflect, giving us an *Annie Hall*-style trip down her memory lane. Via deadpan recollections tinged with humour and mope, we visit a more layered dating scene for the mature queer millennial. As she picks up boys on OkCupid who say things like 'my art defies labels', and chic femmes at gay rights groups who try to pay the bill, Shirin's rebound journey gives us a slice of unapologetic bi.

The multiple identities Shirin has to juggle make her a compelling character who cannot be boxed. While coming out to her conservative Persian family is refreshingly void of trauma, she explains it's 'a process' that her white girlfriend needs to respect. And while a threesome with a man and a woman in less careful hands might have fallen into a bisexual stereotype, it's clear that Shirin can still have a preference and not just anyone goes.

After rave reviews and a sleeper-hit success, *Appropriate Behavior* is already a new-age classic that raised the bar for bisexual representation. And after further beaming bi life onto screens in her subsequent show *The Bisexual*, one can only hope the Carrie Bradshaws of this world will finally get the memo.

OTHER ROMCOMS TO BINGE:

SHIVA BABY (2020)
Originally written as a romcom, this anxiety-ridden dark comedy sees Emma Seligman write, direct and play to the strengths of her identity as a Jewish bisexual agent of chaos.

CHASING AMY (1997)
When lesbian Alyssa (Joey Lauren Adams) went off with a man, much of the backlash failed to consider that maybe she was just bi.

CENTRED THE JOY OF WOMEN ... ALL WOMEN

MAGIC MIKE XXL

DIRECTOR: Gregory Jacobs
WRITER: Reid Carolin
YEAR: 2015

Behold, the *real* sequel to *What Women Want* now we all agree it's *not* Mel Gibson. We could get distracted by reasons why this isn't a romantic comedy, or we could appreciate that this film is about heartbroken male strippers (sorry, *male entertainers*) looking for love, who liven up their quest with some very delightful dancing. There's romance. There's comedy. And in being an agent provocateur in the gender politics of 2015, *Magic Mike XXL* lovingly belongs to our now evolved genre.

In this cheeky, delicious snack of a movie that serves the most basic, yet valid, of needs, Channing Tatum (Mike) and chums get the band back together for a pilgrimage to a strippers' convention. As they road trip across America, in a yogurt truck no less, they happen across groups of women who have been cruelly ignored. From the women over 40 who believe they've had their day, to the girl in the gas station who looks like she's never smiled in her life, the boys adopt a mission of pleasing women (yes, all women) in their wake.

If you like the kind of feminism that thrusts in your face, *Magic Mike XXL* is an anthem to the theatrical degree. With well-meaning heart, and muscles you didn't know existed, each chiselled lead elevates the knight in shining armour to someone who's more than just a double-jointed groin, but is emotionally intelligent and actually uses his ears. Addressing as many female anxieties as possible (by unscientifically eavesdropping on conversations in the women's loo ... probably), a cast of inarguably buff and diverse men attempt to soothe women's worries and raise them up for two hours of pure escapist joy. Anything that lasts two hours and tries to appease all women is certainly going to fail, but we'll take it because, you know what? We're starved. Besides, you don't eat a Snickers for its nutritional value – these guys' nuts are covered in caramel and don't you forget it.

While silver-servicing women, *XXL* also did a solid for the dudes. At a time when 'toxic masculinity' was well into the lexicon, here was a healthier vision of what modern masculinity could be. That's present, empathetic, and wanting to give and receive love – possibly the most crucial message that doesn't have to be a fantasy.

OTHER ROMCOMS TO BINGE:

THE BEST MAN HOLIDAY (2013)
Where the women of the original finally get what they deserve: more airtime and their fellas giving them their own R&B lip-sync show.

MAGIC MIKE'S LAST DANCE (2023)
Well, you might as well watch the third one too. Just for research purposes, of course.

GAVE DIMENSION TO SAUDI ARABIAN WOMEN

BARAKAH MEETS BARAKAH

DIRECTOR: Mahmoud Sabbagh
WRITER: Mahmoud Sabbagh
YEAR: 2016

Meet Barakah (Hisham Fageeh) and Barakah (Fatima AlBanawi), whose similarities end at sharing a name. He's a gold-hearted municipal worker who dutifully polices the streets. She's Bibi – an upper-class influential Instagrammer with a lot to say about the state of the world. When drafted in to interfere with her beach-side shoot, his infatuation begins and she's almost intrigued.

In many romcoms the conflict would be the rub of their social class or the fact his wooing techniques are embarrassingly outdated (thongs in heart-shaped boxes – as she points out – are indeed '1980s thinking'). But this is 2016 Saudi Arabia, and their obstructions are far more militant, and through the prism of Saudi's first romantic comedy we gain an insight into the additional barriers of Middle Eastern love. For once, a romcom embraces very real obstacles and this makes us root for the protagonists even more.

In an education to anyone from the West, and a wink to anyone from the Middle East, the couple plot the impossibility of a date where restaurants might be interrupted by prayer time and beaches could be raided. But Barakah informs us that Saudi hasn't always been this restrictive. In two arresting archival vignettes, we see a Jeddah that freely enjoyed culture before the Islamic revival. Girls giggle at school, air stewardesses wear short sleeves and couples

enjoy the cinemas before their closure in 1979. As Barakah laments his father's free-spirited generation, he suggests how media can be a force for reinvention, cutting to Bibi wrangling a selfie while carefully cropping out her eyes.

Bibi's character is a revolution for anyone with assumptions about Saudi women. Using social media, she delivers messages of activism and, before the religious police break up her art gallery meet-cute, she makes it clear she's no 'bimbo' while schooling Barakah on conceptual art.

Since her role as the frank, forthright and cosmopolitan Bibi, Saudi-born Fatima AlBanawi has challenged the stigmas that often see Middle Eastern men as terrorists and women as suppressed. With a Harvard doctorate in Theological Studies, she's observed how art – even a romcom – can change hearts and minds, which drew the first-time actress to this foundational role. This is where *Barakah Meets Barakah* is romantic comedy at its most powerful – marrying a hopeful romance with meaningful social commentary.

OTHER ROMCOMS TO BINGE:

HALAL LOVE (AND SEX) (2015)
Four stories set in Beirut, one common theme – navigating love while adhering to their faith.

CARAMEL (2007)
Another luminous, and award-winning, romcom, this time liberating the lives of five individual Lebanese women.

SHOWED GOING IT ALONE
WAS THE RIGHT WAY TO GO

HOW TO BE SINGLE

DIRECTOR: Christian Ditter
WRITERS: Abby Kohn, Marc Silverstein, Dana Fox
YEAR: 2016

There's a whole market geared towards the anti-Valentine's Day agenda, which some will feel grateful for when not feeling the love. *How to Be Single* is for those mystified, burnt or plain bored by love, and explores a series of scenarios that buck the lovey-dovey trend. But what's most refreshing about this 2016 Valentine's Day release is the underscored truth that you can totally go it alone.

How to Be Single isn't exactly a manual – more a peek into the lives of a randy bunch of New Yorkers. Across a cast as long as a weekly shopping list, insights on contemporary coupledom are prodded with tongue-in-cheek charm. But among the sub-stories of cracking dating-site algorithms or choosing a sperm donor, our most resonant lessons are learnt by Alice (Dakota Johnson) and Robin (Rebel Wilson). Here are two examples of how to do life in the single lane where it's made to look (eventually) like an actual life hack. OK, so Alice doesn't quite realize that flying solo is what she needs straight away, but there's poetry in her journey of finding that out for herself. As she tells us in that romcom boilerplate voiceover, 'This story isn't about relationships. It's about all those times in between when maybe, just maybe, our real life is happening.'

Meanwhile, Robin's idea of a long-term relationship is anyone who stays long enough to brush their teeth in her sink. As too many films see women who behave like this as dysfunctional (even Amy Schumer's *Trainwreck* fell on that sword), it's liberating to see Robin unashamedly having fun, while wisely telling Alice to avoid the 'dicksand'. Leslie Mann's character does fly dangerously close to the 'all women want kids' crap, but there's feminism too in knowing that women change their minds. Yet, her resolute decision to go straight to the sperm bank at least subtly highlights the choices we now have.

How to Be Single shows how you can rely on yourself, and a relationship with the wrong person can be the loneliest thing. And as Alice sentimentally looks over the mountain she's just climbed, she reminds us to 'cherish' those times where you really stand alone. Besides, who knows how long it will last.

OTHER ROMCOMS TO BINGE:

AN UNMARRIED WOMAN (1978)
The poster says it all: 'After her divorce Erica got to know some pretty interesting people, including herself'.

EAT PRAY LOVE (2010)
The one that made eating carbs and travelling alone the done thing when you're dumped.

THE LOBSTER (2015)
A dystopian black-comedy twist to the apparent absurdity of being single. Ingenious.

WAS AN UNAPOLOGETIC ODE TO A BLACK FEMALE EXPERIENCE

GIRLS TRIP

DIRECTOR: Malcolm D. Lee
WRITERS: Kenya Barris,
Erica Rivinoja, Tracy Oliver
YEAR: 2017

While *Sex and the City* and *Bridesmaids* filled the gap for ladies to be unladylike, Hollywood's neglect of an outrageous group of Black women had become a gaping hole. Thankfully, Regina Hall, Queen Latifah, Tiffany Haddish and Jada Pinkett Smith brought the 'Flosse Posse' to the party, because why should white women get all the fun?

While many can relate to the four personalities of boss lady Sasha, finicky mother Lisa, workaholic wife Ryan or wild child Dina, *Girls Trip* made specific efforts to be unapologetically Black. Sleeping in silk hair wraps, clocking Maxwell singing on stage (having probably conceived some babies to his album *Urban Hang Suite*) and wondering how Larenz Tate from *Love Jones* is still so *fyne* will be uniquely recognizable to Black women north of 40.

And where better to set the stage for a celebration of Black womanhood than a festival hosted by *Essence*? Since 1970 the glossy magazine has been the American Black woman's style bible after recognizing they were an overlooked demographic. Unfortunately, being overlooked is something Black women are both used to and tired of, making *Girls Trip* such a relief. At last we could relax into an escapist comedy about relationships that wasn't about suffering or being a sidekick.

The last time grown Black women featured in a mainstream romantic comedy was 1995, in the screen adaptation of Terry McMillan's *Waiting to Exhale*. And proving *Girls Trip* recognizes the shoulders it stands on, McMillan is just one of the iconic female cameos alongside idols Ava DuVernay, Mariah Carey and MC Lyte. In addition to bowing down to icons *Girls Trip* also polished the rising star of Tiffany Haddish. Through her sexually rabid character Dina, she showed what one can do with a banana and a grapefruit, putting a whole new meaning to breakfast at Tiffany's.

Girls Trip became the first Black-led movie to gross a $100m box office, dispelling the myth that Black stories don't connect with wide audiences. The fact that crowds came to see 'The Flosse Posse' en masse strengthened a message within the most meaningful romcoms: people are most attractive when being true to themselves.

OTHER ROMCOMS TO BINGE:

WAITING TO EXHALE (1995, SEE PAGE 66)
The ultimate blockbusting romance where Black women and their friendships ruled.

JUMPING THE BROOM (2011)
Taking the historical African-American tradition of hopping over a broom, here's an unapologetically Black romcom that's hailed as a classic.

GAVE TOXIC MASCULINITY
A DRESSING-DOWN

PHANTOM THREAD

DIRECTOR: Paul Thomas Anderson
WRITERS: Paul Thomas Anderson
YEAR: 2017

Before we delve into how this film explores toxic masculinity, let's not forget to check its romantic comedy ID. Granted, the exquisite direction from Paul Thomas Anderson might be a departure from the typical romcom, but with its deranged romance and barbed humour, it belongs in the genre while pulling up its socks. Besides, what's more entertaining than hearing posh people spit 'fuck off' at each other while using poisonous mushroom omelettes as tantric-sex foreplay?

Talking of Paul Thomas Anderson, it's time we appreciate him as a masquerading romcom connoisseur: in *Boogie Nights, Punch-Drunk Love, Inherent Vice* and *Licorice Pizza*, his work has always been buoyed with screwball humour and dysfunctional love. But while critics may laud PTA as a hero, it's his romcom-queen wife Maya Rudolph who really inspired the tale, as after the fastidious director found himself sick in her care, he was compelled to explore the power balance of couples in love.

Set in 1950s London and in a mansion for a cage, Reynolds Woodcock, a distinguished couturier with a banquet of demands, lures clumsy Alma from waitress to muse. After wooing her with a decadent breakfast order that reads like a shopping list, we know he's a 'hungry boy' who expects women to feed his needs. He

fits her with a dress and she apologizes for having no breasts, so he tells her it's 'his job' to give her some – that is, 'if I choose'.

It's this seething manipulation and privileged expectations that sour this bewitching relationship, which smacks of toxic male behaviour – but like the embroidery she stitches in yet another elegant gown, Alma is delicate yet sharp and ends up glowing with revenge. Falling sick, Woodcock finds himself uncharacteristically vulnerable, and eventually Alma has her lover in the palm of her hand. Maybe now he won't bark at her for buttering her toast too loudly, because he no longer has the strength to live up to his apt surname. As they both get a kick out of the shift in power, a new dynamic is formed that works for them both. And for those who want a little BDSM in their romcoms, you can get your kicks in Alma, who wants Woodcock 'helpless, tender, open, with only me to help'.

OTHER ROMCOMS TO BINGE:

PUNCH-DRUNK LOVE (2002)
Adam Sandler gained some major cred in this exquisite romance about one man, his seven sisters and a desperate bout of loneliness.

HUMPDAY (2009)
Lynn Shelton's uncomfortably hilarious comedy about two straight men who dare to make a gay porno. One-up-manship never looked so ridiculous.

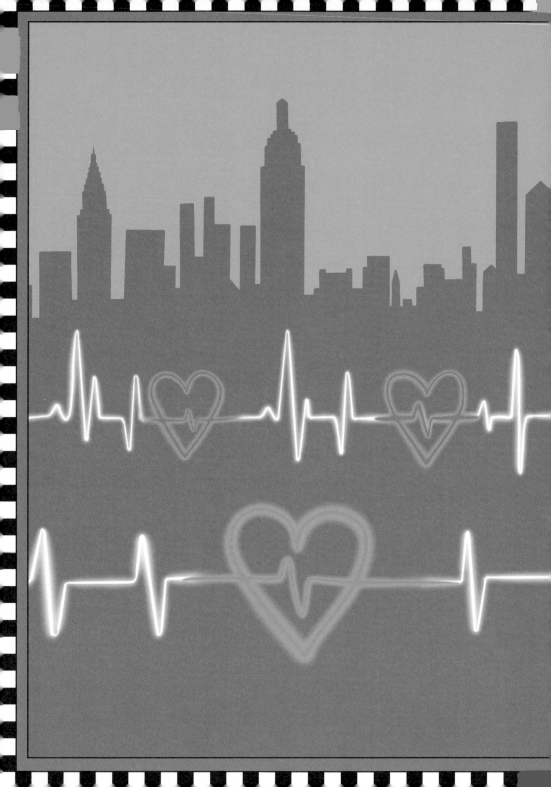

HAD A HEALTHIER MOTHER-DAUGHTER RELATIONSHIP

THE BIG SICK

DIRECTOR: Michael Showalter
WRITERS: Emily V. Gordon, Kumail Nanjiani
YEAR: 2017

Within the heightened world of typical romantic comedies, parents are portrayed as being the butt of most jokes. From overprotective dads in denial that their daughters have a vagina, to prim and fussy mothers who have a habit of reminding them their eggs are about to shrivel up. It's why 2017's The Big Sick felt like a spoonful of medicine for healthier mother-daughter relationships that weren't awkward or mean – and in witnessing two related women who don't just love, but also like each other, the tide for maternal relationships began to see a turn.

Against the backdrop of Trump-empowered Islamophobia that swelled in 2017, this was the romcom the world needed. Lifted from the real-world meet-cute of Pakistani-American comedian Kumail Nanjiani and his white American wife Emily V. Gordon – who really did shout 'woo hoo!' during one of his gigs – a story of navigating interracial relationships within angsty America gave the genre of romcoms a contemporary edge. Emily (played by Zoe Kazan) finds herself in a coma when dating a guy she only half knows, and while this means she spends most of the film comatose, in steps her mother Beth (Holly Hunter) to fight her corner in every way.

As Emily lies unconscious, Kumail learns a lot from her mother and observes lessons in honesty, integrity and people's ability to forgive. And after being dumped for not being honest about his family's attempts to find him a Pakistani wife, Kumail finds himself armed with the emotional tools he'll need if Emily ever wakes up. The subplot of Beth's journey, from defensive solidarity with her daughter to evolving compassion – considering the cultural context in which Kumail's selective truths are exposed – unfolds as a nuanced tale of a mother's desire for her child's happiness and her acceptance of people as fallible, especially when they have the potential to make her daughter happy.

All this isn't a mother wrapping her daughter in any cliché cotton wool, as after Emily's rehabilitation Beth knows it's time for her to leave. And even though Emily says she's not ready to be alone, she tells her, 'You're strong. And you are', confident in the knowledge that's the kind of woman she's raised.

OTHER ROMCOMS TO BINGE:

MAMMA MIA! (2008, SEE PAGE 134)
OK, so it's a little weird that the daughter doesn't get more of a ticking off for reading her mum's sex diary, but you get the point.

KISSING JESSICA STEIN (2001, SEE PAGE 104)
When Jessica's mother makes it clear she doesn't care if her daughter is gay, it more than makes up for the fact she spends the movie trying to marry her off to random guys.

BROUGHT A 'COCO QUEEN' TO THE ROMCOM PARTY

THE INCREDIBLE JESSICA JAMES

DIRECTOR: Jim Strouse
WRITER: Jim Strouse
YEAR: 2017

An image search of 'romcom heroine' paints a very telling picture: Julia Roberts, Cameron Diaz, Sandra Bullock, Audrey Hepburn, Katherine Heigl, Meg Ryan ... Glittering results that compete for the biggest doe-eyed smile. While worthy of such titles, they could inspire a #RomcomsSoWhite campaign. This is why Jessica James (Jessica Williams) isn't just incredible, but also signified change.

Twenty-something Jessica has no hesitation in referring to herself as 'tall, pretty, smart and obviously a coco queen', but not before turning that romcom screw of dancing like no one's watching across a twinkling New York sky. Sure, we've seen this trope before, but in the arena of quirky leading ladies, Jessica is the new Black.

Refreshingly, however, her skin colour has nothing to do with the plot. Nor is it the fact that she dates both white (Chris O'Dowd) and Black (LaKeith Stanfield) men. In an authentic depiction of cosmopolitan New York, interracial dating is a thing, and nobody gives a damn. Instead, they are more concerned with issues that actually deserve headspace, such as Boone's (O'Dowd) divorce and whether Jessica's going to fulfil her ambition of becoming a playwright.

With Jessica's professional dreams at the heart of her motivations, she's so much more than just a lovelorn lead. She's unapologetically feminist (don't let her catch you manspreading on the subway!), and embraces her post-break-up 'weird transitional phase' by swiping through Tinder dates and confiding in her white lesbian BFF (another flipped script from the Black best-friend trope). As for the stream of theatre-company rejection letters, she recycles them as motivational wallpaper in a lesson to us all on utilizing disappointment.

Black women romcom stars haven't always been missing in action. The 1990s and early 2000s boom of Black Hollywood was a love-in of bougie crowd-pleasers which saw Nia Long, Sanaa Lathan, Vivica A. Fox, Jada Pinkett Smith and Vanessa Williams on repeat. But try an image search of those actresses and you'll see that many are as fair-skinned as their hair is straight. Jessica Williams, owning her dreads, nose ring and that 'coco queen' skin is a vision of realness and plants another rose in the bouquet of what beautiful can be.

OTHER ROMCOMS TO BINGE:

THE LOVEBIRDS (2020)
Issa Rae and Kumail Nanjiani provide a dynamite duo where their interracial relationship is the least of their worries.

CORRINA, CORRINA (1994)
The one where Whoopi Goldberg chipped away at the Black maid stereotype while breaking down barriers for interracial romance.

WAS AN ODE TO INDEPENDENT WOMEN

CRAZY RICH ASIANS

DIRECTOR: Jon M. Chu
WRITERS: Peter Chiarelli, Adele Lim, Kevin Kwan
YEAR: 2018

Crazy Rich Asians didn't just end a 25-year drought of Hollywood films to feature an all-Asian cast (the last being 1993's *The Joy Luck Club*), but it also revived the romcom with a new feminist spin. Lifting the roles from the 2013 book, it rallied a bevy of women who possessed power, integrity and independence to form an inspiring team.

In this film that circles the relationship of Rachel, an American-born Chinese, and Singapore-born Nick, women rule, wearing various crowns. Ah Ma is the matriarch to the wealthy Young family; Rachel's single mother Kerry and Nick's mother Eleanor (whose husband is never seen) raise their kids to understand graft, ambition and tradition in context to both their Asian and American cultures. When Nick's family wedding sees him travel home from New York, we also meet ethereal cousin Astrid, who's a millionaire philanthropist.

Elevating the Cinderella story, economics professor Rachel had no idea she was basically dating a prince. Once the penny's dropped, she's more irked than bedazzled, as she's smart enough to know that all that glitters is not gold. When she realizes she can't let herself marry a man whose mother says she will 'never be enough', a power move of integrity helps the disapproving Eleanor see herself in Rachel as someone who stands

for what she believes – even if it does translate differently from one continent and generation to the next. It's a relief to see nuance applied to the 'mean ol' mother-in-law' trope, as Eleanor (Michelle Yeoh) could otherwise be read as a conniving ice-queen. But her actions are given a biting backstory, letting us know she had to prove her worth to make it to the top.

The side story of Astrid is satisfying and curt. When she hides her shopping-spree booty from her 'commoner' husband, we learn his fragile masculinity can't handle a woman who wears the 'money pants'. While it's frustrating to see a woman hide treats she's entitled to enjoy, our disappointment melts when she dumps him, saying, 'It's not my job to make you feel like a man. I can't make you something you're not.'

Lessons in dignity run through each of these women, as none of them are afraid to go it alone. And as the world finally woke up to recognize the value in authentic Asian stories, these women raised the bar for others, who always knew their worth.

OTHER ROMCOMS TO BINGE:

ALWAYS BE MY MAYBE (2019, SEE PAGE 186)
Bringing the American-Asian romcom a bit more down to earth, a slightly less fantastical love story.

THE JOY LUCK CLUB (1993)
For paving the way for *Crazy Rich Asians,* this celebrated mother–daughter melodrama deserves its dues.

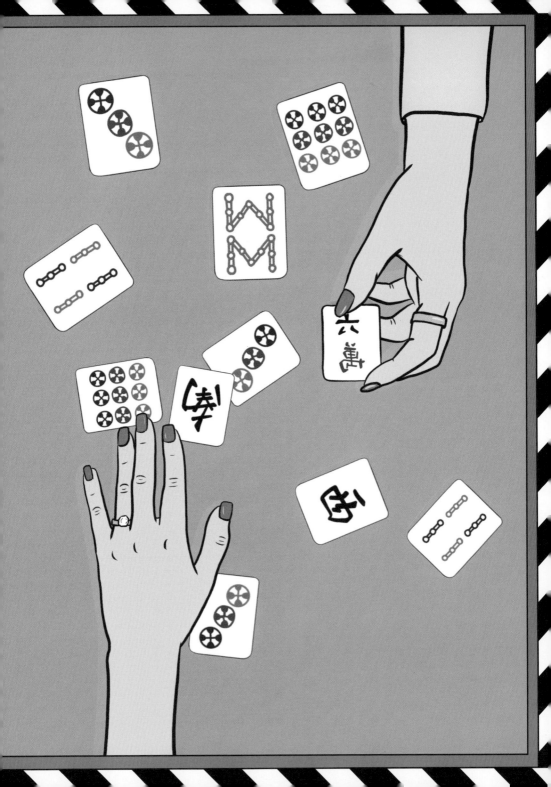

OPENED UP HONEST CONVERSATIONS ABOUT IVF

PRIVATE LIFE

DIRECTOR: Tamara Jenkins
WRITER: Tamara Jenkins
YEAR: 2018

Private Life sees 40-something married couple Rachel (Kathryn Hahn) and Richard (Paul Giamatti) navigate an expensive pilgrimage to parenthood. When an adoption falls through and Richard's one testicle isn't performing, they approach Richard's stepbrother's free-spirited daughter, who agrees to lend them her eggs. She's not biologically related (see 'stepbrother'), so the procedure goes forth, but not without a slew of family judgement and the drama that comes with injecting a 25-year-old with hormones. Thanks to this romantic comedy, IVF is painfully hilarious.

By blending wit as dry as sandpaper to the rare representation of trying for a family in your forties, the film prods necessary conversations on work vs parenthood for women in artistic careers. Drawing from the experiences of director Tamara Jenkins' own pool of friends, she portrays the reality of how, for many female artists, finally making enough to feed an extra mouth collides with dwindling fertility and the harsh realization that biology is no feminist.

Within the many poignant lines, weary Rachel talks of being 'betrayed' by feminist ideology: 'That lie that I could have a career and kids. I should send them the bill for our IVF!' But this stinging provocation, which reads as a stiff finger up at a world that has allowed this injustice to happen, is soon lifted by another of Richard's droll lines: 'You can't blame second-wave feminism for our ambivalence to having a kid.' Sadie, representing the younger generation of aspiring artists born into yet another round of socio-economic drudgery, wades into this political bone of contention: 'I don't want a child, I want a career.' How are we still in a place where having it all is just something you post on Instagram?

Private Life ushered in a sophisticated maturity to romantic comedies. With the topic of fertility so ripe for tender storytelling, it's a wonder it's so rarely embraced for its dramatic appeal. From exhilarating highs and crushing lows, to the comic relief of spending the day masturbating into a cup, making babies and facing the options society has given women to do so could be just what the next generation of romcom fans needs.

OTHER ROMCOMS TO BINGE:

BABY MAMA (2008)
Who hasn't thought about how wonderful it would be if Tina Fey and Amy Poehler's chemistry came to the point of procreation?

GOOD NEWWZ (2019)
In this highest-grossing Hindu-language film of 2019, mislabelled sperm causes insemination chaos.

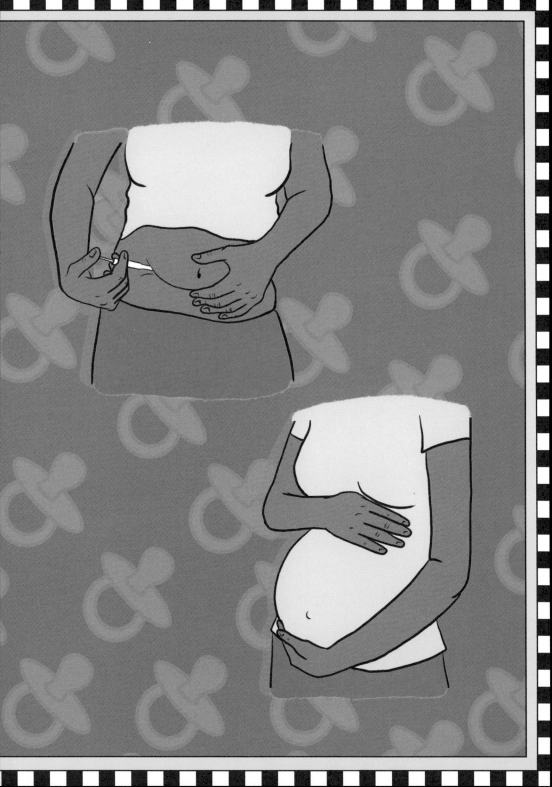

CALLED OUT
WORKPLACE INEQUALITY

SET IT UP

DIRECTOR: Claire Scanlon
WRITER: Katie Silberman
YEAR: 2018

Women who have to work their way up in the world will recognize the Easter eggs of grind scattered throughout *Set It Up*. Always eating on the job? Well, canapés are cheaper than buying dinner. Ever stolen the office toilet paper? Who has time to buy supplies when you're constantly working overtime?

In this perceptive romcom for the Netflix generation, personal assistant Harper embodies the aspirational struggle of creative women in the corporate world. In *Set It Up* we meet burnt-out personal assistants Harper and Charlie as they tend to their ball-busting bosses Kirsten and Rick. In their integral meet-cute, which sees one takeaway meal vs two assistants with a hungry CEO, Harper snaps, 'You won't get fired, you'll just swoop in with your lacrosse stick and fraternity connections and keep getting promoted for no reason.' Despite her ambitions, Harper knows she's in a world that favours white men in suits and will have to try that bit harder just to stay afloat.

While Harper represents a woman hustling up, her boss Kirsten embodies the clench of responsibility of women who broke the glass ceiling. Steely Kirsten is the online publishing version of *The Devil Wears Prada's* Miranda Priestly. However, for a woman of colour working in a male-dominated sports world –

reporting on topics such as lesbian Nigerian women's football – her success is harder won and more slippery to hold.

To aspiring writer Harper, Kirsten's scowl will never be more intimidating than the glare of her blank page, and we're reminded there's only so long you can put off a dream before it keeps you up at night. Yet, in a nod to today's unsustainable work-life imbalance, Harper tells Rick, 'After working so hard I've got no energy to actually write anything.'

For strapped workers like Harper, quitting to pursue ambition isn't an option. But in this script from Katie Silberman (whose work includes feminist manifesto movies *Booksmart* and *Isn't It Romantic*), it's when she's unfairly sacked that she's finally free to write. With the glow of accomplishment, Harper's all the more appealing and Charlie decides that selling his soul to an unethical boss is not for him. He quits, they kiss and Charlie knows – as anyone who faces structural inequality already does – that most things are better when they are earned.

OTHER ROMCOMS TO BINGE:

**HOW TO LOSE A GUY IN 10 DAYS
(2003, SEE PAGE 118)**
Aka 'How to Realize You're in the Wrong Job in 10 Days'.

THE HATING GAME (2021)
A tug of war over ethics vs professional success for two colleagues who hate to love each other.

VALIDATED THE EMOTIONS OF TEENAGE GIRLS

TO ALL THE BOYS I'VE LOVED BEFORE

DIRECTOR: Susan Johnson
WRITERS: Jenny Han, Sofia Alvarez
YEAR: 2018

There's a reason why young adult novels make great film adaptations: they provide fertile ground for first-time feels. And while the prickles of puppy love are rarely taken seriously, Jenny Han's novels validate these enormous emotions that engulf the average teen.

Han's *To All the Boys* pays a rare respect to a coming-of-age story where a young girl is learning to negotiate her head and heart. When 16-year-old Lara Jean writes letters to all the boys she's loved with no intention of sending them, it's a perfectly healthy way to offload while avoiding the horror of rejection. Of course, these letters find their way to their recipients, thanks to the meddling of her younger sister (more on her in a minute), but although drowned in the despair of such a catastrophe, it's portrayed as a fast track to maturity when she learns the power of confrontation and rising above.

As *Crazy Rich Asians* burst a dam for Asian representation on the big screen, *To All the Boys* (released the same week) beamed into millions of homes with a Netflix account. Adapted from Korean-American Jenny Han's ninth book, here was another win for mainstream representation of Asian-American women – this time centring the universal theme of impassioned teenage spirit.

Although young adult novels have long been adapted for screen, girls who looked like *Twilight's* Bella, *Harry Potter's* Hermione and *Hunger Games'* Katniss were the only ones who got to shine. This radically changed when Lara Jean came along and, as Han agreed to go with the only production company that would not whitewash her story, a new Asian-American heroine was born.

Lara's sagacious character provides quite the girl boss, but it's 11-year-old sister Kitty who literally wears the 'feminist' necklace. With her belief that girls should make the first move (hence the letters), riffing on the feminist ideology of the moon and rejection of a bridesmaid's dress for a tux. If this is the shape of our young women to come, things are looking up.

OTHER ROMCOMS TO BINGE:

XO, KITTY (2023)
For more of that Kitty energy now she's come of age.

THE HALF OF IT (2020)
More letter-writing high jinks with this sweet coming-of-age romcom that sees Ellie Chu take a shine to girls.

THE DIARY OF A TEENAGE GIRL (2015)
Being slapped with an 18 rating for its depiction of a 15-year-old girl exploring sex said a lot about our anxieties around young girls' sexuality.

PROVED SUCCESSFUL WOMEN CAN BE LOVED

ALWAYS BE MY MAYBE

DIRECTOR: Nahnatchka Khan
WRITERS: Ali Wong, Randall Park, Michael Golamco
YEAR: 2019

Here are some things that romcoms are accused of peddling: 1) a successful woman can't possibly be loveable, as their ambition will always come first; 2) women can't have a career, as finding love is akin to handing in their resignation. While we're at it, and for a bonus point: 3) to be cast in a romcom you need to be white and wear contacts, as no woman would wear glasses post-makeover scene.

This is what makes *Always Be My Maybe* such a pleasing new horizon. In this Netflix hit by an all-Asian-American team, Ali Wong and Randall Park play childhood friends who become lovers, with some empowering twists. After clumsily losing their virginity in the back of a car, Sasha (Wong) and Marcus (Park) awkwardly lose touch. But after a 15-year hiatus, they conveniently reconvene when jobbing rapper Marcus installs the now high-flying celebrity chef Sasha's air-con. Without giving the game away – but, yes, you guessed right – they end up in love because that's what romcoms do. But going back to points 1), 2) and 3), this film gets there differently, rimmed glasses and all.

A class clash is always ripe for a romcom theme, but seeing Marcus finally get to grips with Sasha's success is as satisfying as seeing Sasha go for 'a regular guy'. She doesn't need Marcus to be *the* Keanu Reeves (in one of the most bizarre romcom cameos ever) or as high-flying as her ex-fiancé Brandon, who was using her to elevate his brand. But when she tells Marcus, 'I don't need you to live my life, but I need you to understand that this is my life,' he is faced with a moment of possible emasculation. Yet, with progressive stripes that don't perpetuate toxic masculinity, he's just a guy, standing in front of a girl, asking to (literally) hold her purse.

After the glamour of *Crazy Rich Asians*, here was another Asian-American cast romcom, but with a more grounded approach. With Wong and Park's wish to write an 'Asian *When Harry Met Sally*', they landed a story stuffed with culturally specific nodes wrapped in the universal tale of love. Meanwhile, in this vision of what a supportive partner can look like, women can believe there's room for love at the top.

OTHER ROMCOMS TO BINGE:

LONG SHOT (2019, SEE PAGE 192)
Proving 2019 was the year of knowing that behind every great woman, was a man willing to change his name (or hold the purse).

HIS GIRL FRIDAY (1940, SEE PAGE 24)
Where Hildy's passion and talent for journalism was what Walter loved most. Rosalind Russell and Cary Grant at their finest.

GAVE INDIA ITS FIRST MAINSTREAM LESBIAN ROMANCE

HOW I FELT WHEN I SAW THAT GIRL
(EK LADKI KO DEKHA TOH AISA LAGA)

DIRECTOR: Shelly Chopra Dhar
WRITERS: Shelly Chopra Dhar, Gazal Dhaliwal, P.G. Wodehouse
YEAR: 2019

In the opening scenes of *How I Felt When I Saw That Girl* we're invited to a joyous al fresco wedding. Pastel petals and glittering saris whirl among the elated guests united in synchronized dance. Love is in the air and in the heart-shaped jalebi. With weddings being hunting grounds for matchmaking possibilities, Kuhu shimmies over to Sweety to sing her brother's praises with a glint in her eye. So far, so Bollywood.

Audiences would have been forgiven for expecting what followed to involve some husband-finding high jinks for Sweety. But come the intermission (because Bollywood films are long), director Shelly Chopra Dhar had taken India down a path of enlightenment, with Sweety and Kuhu's cunning coming-out tale.

Just a year after India decriminalized homosexuality, *How I Felt When I Saw That Girl* was released. It gave Chopra Dhar (mother to a gay son) and Gazal Dhaliwal (a trans woman), licence to breathe compassion, using the propellers of mainstream Bollywood.

With India's only other major lesbian film – 1996's *Fire* – seeing cinemas vandalized in protest both for and against its release, Dhar knew she had to tread on careful ground and abide by conventional audience expectations if she was going to tackle a society still warming to same-sex love. By centring the first half of the story on male protagonists, avoiding any girl-on-girl romance in the marketing, and casting Bollywood's biggest stars, Dhar attracted a crowd with the potential to swap a small mind with a big heart.

This gentle hoodwinking is wired into the film's plot, giving it a savvy meta twist. When Sweety's true identity is smuggled into a play written by her initial love interest (he soon accepts he's barking up the wrong tree), the play is performed to an audience who are then forced to either face their prejudice or succumb to a beautiful love story.

This refreshing romantic comedy has brought Bollywood up to date by seasoning a stew of Indian romcoms with the spice of inclusivity. With its mounting success leading it to stream worldwide on Netflix, Shelly Chopra Dhar helped make lesbian romance as mainstream as a high-street madras.

OTHER ROMCOMS TO BINGE:

SHUBH MANGAL ZYADA SAAVDHAN (2020)
Annnd one year later came the Bollywood romcom for gay guys.

BEND IT LIKE BECKHAM (2002, SEE PAGE 108)
Anyone not picking up on the lesbian tendencies here needs to polish their gaydar.

KNEW LOVING YOURSELF ALWAYS COMES FIRST

ISN'T IT ROMANTIC

DIRECTOR: Todd Strauss-Schulson
WRITERS: Erin Cardillo,
Dana Fox, Katie Silberman
YEAR: 2019

Meet Natalie (Rebel Wilson), our cynical hero who's got Venn diagrams at the ready on why romcoms suck. Despite her best friend's protests that they remind us of how lovely life can be, Nat has a longer list of why they really get her goat. As she offloads the problematics of the typical tropes, we realize she's making quite a convincing case. And who can blame her when the romcoms she's seen routinely overlook women who look like her as a lead? Her mother forewarned her: 'They don't make movies about girls like us,' as she sat as a doe-eyed child in front of *Pretty Woman* on VHS.

When Natalie's in a 48-hour coma, she's confronted by an alternate reality where you can park in sunlit New York with ridiculous ease. But before she discovers the way to magic herself home, we get a satirical romp into how daft romcoms can be. From the gay best friend 'who sets gay rights back 100 years' to waking up 'beguiling' with a full face of Mac, *Isn't It Romantic* gets increasingly sarcastic as our pleasure in the genre becomes guilty as charged.

The suggestion that Wilson as a lead could only be achieved in a fantasy is an issue in itself and prods us to think about how unacceptable that is. In an objective that flirts with being a little too obvious, the goal is still scored with some delectable grace: you can't say 'I love you' until you love yourself first and the only person who can complete you is ... you.

Wilson found herself soon apologizing after claiming to be 'the first plus-sized girl' to be a romcom star. In fact, Black women had long before broken this ground but with the films of Mo'Nique and Queen Latifah often swept into a 'Black' film category (if you count skin colour as a genre), it's a reminder to anyone who thinks romcoms lack depth or positive representation, when in fact there are plenty of gems waiting to prove them wrong.

OTHER ROMCOMS TO BINGE:

THEY CAME TOGETHER (2014)
Four stories set in Beirut, one common theme – navigating love while hurdling faith. Charming, progressive and hilarious.

JUST WRIGHT (2010)
The plus-size romcom royal still reigns as Queen Latifah. Kudos for founding a production company and casting herself across some of the finest Black men. In *Last Holiday* it was LL Cool J, here it's Common.

THE BROKEN HEARTS GALLERY (2020)
Where energetic Gen-Zs, such as Geraldine Viswanathan, reignite the romcom with young women with grit.

ILLUSTRATED THE CHALLENGES FOR WOMEN IN POLITICS

LONG SHOT

DIRECTOR: Jonathan Levine
WRITERS: Dan Sterling, Liz Hannah
YEAR: 2019

Remember the pandemonium when Michelle Obama casually bared her arms in public, or when Diane Abbott had a cheeky can of mojito on public transport? And can you believe the vicious comparisons to a 'bin racoon' that Alexandria Ocasio-Cortez's boyfriend received when he didn't fit people's idea of who she should date? These real-life examples of how the world treats women politicians are the premise of *Long Shot*.

As the title toys with our internalized bias of how 'mismatched' Charlize Theron and Seth Rogen are, it's also suggestive of how much harder women need to bat in the political field. In contrast we meet Fred (Rogen) – a schlubby keyboard warrior journalist who exercises his freedom to say and do as he pleases. When his loose lips and tight principles see him quit his job, he finds himself writing speeches for his former babysitter crush Charlotte, who's now running for office. Despite her childhood dreams of placing the environment's decline high on the political agenda, her staff are more focused on keeping her likeability score high. This means working on her wave and avoiding eating anything on a stick, rather than her policies on saving Mother Earth.

It's when Fred brings his idealism to the table that we really see the rub. She tells him, 'If I'm angry, I'm hysterical. If I'm emotional, I'm weak.

If I so much as raise my voice, I'm a bitch.' These are words that will ring truer to women less Aryan than Theron. And when an R-rated catastrophe sees his webcam history leaked, she solemnly reminds him: 'The woman who stands beside the guy that's cumming on his face gets way more scrutiny than the guy who's actually cumming on his face.' Preach.

While women may be inching towards more legislative power, *Long Shot* reminds us that post-feminism is a myth – something that still resonates in a world where Kamala Harris has a set of keys to the White House. In a metric that's more mandatory for women than men, 'likeability' points are gained the more 'feminine' they are. But when that same research shows people don't equate femininity to 'leader', women remain in a place more unsettling than Fred's 13-year-old erection.

OTHER ROMCOMS TO BINGE:

THE AMERICAN PRESIDENT (1995)
If 'politics is perception', here's a suited Annette Bening, us the president's girlfriend, taking no shit.

HAV PLENTY (1998)
For another example of a high-class woman retaining her lifestyle, despite 'dating down'.

THE PARTY (2017)
However will a newly elected politician deal with the demise of her 30-year marriage? A comedy of manners that's far more fun than it sounds.

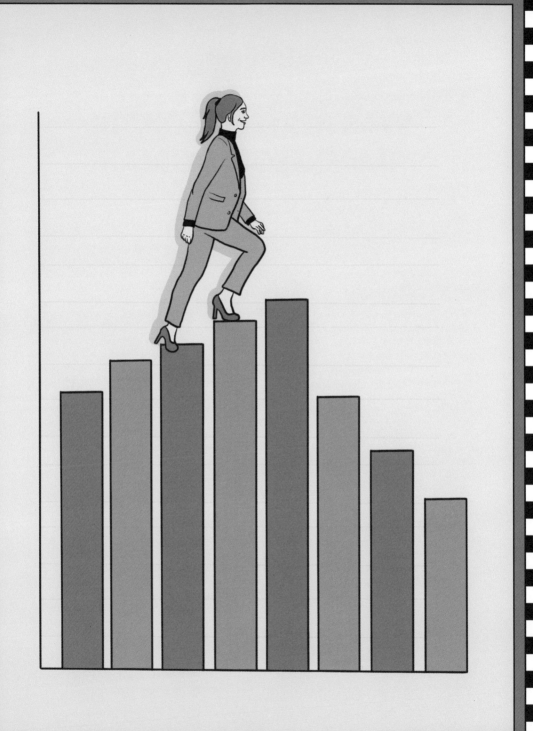

WAS PERFECT FOR THE IMPERFECT WOMAN

PLUS ONE

DIRECTOR: Jeff Chan, Andrew Rhymer
WRITERS: Jeff Chan, Andrew Rhymer
YEAR: 2019

This critic-adored indie banger sees two singletons attend an intimidating calendar of nuptials as each other's plus one. Although this scenario might feel like a bout of déjà vu, there's refinement in Maya Erskine's Alice, who's imperfect, inappropriate and badass – and helped romcoms feel brand new.

In this observant romantic comedy, the facade of 'ladylike' is trashed, while respectability politics are probed. Alice ruptures decorous ideas often expected of women (and Asian-American women at that) by living unapologetically in a way that makes high-school friend Ben (Jack Quaid) squirm. We're talking peeing in the shower, getting her 'cooter' out in a cemetery and shaming Ben when he's a dick. This may not be how Ben had imagined his fantasy woman, but it makes Alice human and more tangible than some dream, and in rejecting normcore social expectations – even more exasperating within the rigid rituals of weddings – she reminds us that each woman lives by her own rules.

Bursting the bubble on what the perfect relationship looks like, *Plus One* brought home some truth to an age of tech-inspired idealism. With millennials entering adulthood alongside the dating-app boom, the suffocation of choice made decisions on life partners more stifling. Suddenly, it was too easy to let lovers go, as we could swipe to the next without realizing we'd already struck gold, which is of course what Ben foolishly does to Alice once their relationship evolves. It would've been too easy for Alice to bend to Ben's whim or beg, so instead she tells him to do one and gets back with her ex.

With romcoms being guilty of fashioning unrealistic ideals, here's one that takes some responsibility, with pragmatism in its bones. In a golden noble moment Ben is schooled by his happily married buddy that no one's ever *really* sure. In this world obsessed with evaluating everything, overthinking is futile with the irrationality of the heart, and besides 'when you find someone you want to hang out with as long as humanly possible' maybe call off the search?

Alice isn't perfect, as that just doesn't exist, but she's certainly exceptional, which is a healthier concept to crave.

OTHER ROMCOMS TO BINGE:

BRIDGET JONES'S DIARY (2001, SEE PAGE 102)
For wearing feminine ideals like an itchy pair of tights, Bridget Jones became an unlikely icon.

THE BIG SICK (2017, SEE PAGE 174)
She would have been perfect, if only she was from Pakistan. Here the 'wrong' girl turned out to be right.

WHEN HARRY MET SALLY (1989, SEE PAGE 54)
The original for unapologetically owning her high-maintenance low maintenance.

194

PROVED A WOMAN'S HERITAGE IS WHERE HER HEART IS

TOP END WEDDING

DIRECTOR: Wayne Blair
WRITERS: Miranda Tapsell, Joshua Tyler, Glen Condie
YEAR: 2019

Aboriginal women haven't had much love under the romcom gazebo, so it's welcome to see writer Miranda Tapsell star in this aisle. While inviting us along to her wedding caper, which sees a mad dash to organize a wedding in 10 days in the Northern Territory of Australia, *Top End Wedding* reminds us how integral a woman's heritage is to her identity.

While besotted with the chemistry between Lauren and Ned, the real love story lies within Lauren's relationship to her aboriginal roots. It's a side to her that she serendipitously explores while on a mission to track down her mother, who may or may not have run off with a French pilot. During an existential road trip careering from her hometown in Darwin to her mother's ancestral land in Tiwi, she discovers aspects of her culture she's finally ready to embrace. It's not that she's been disinterested before, but rather that there's not been much time, while busy climbing a ladder within a successful legal career.

Momentarily calling off the wedding because Ned lied about leaving his job conveniently frees Lauren to do the last leg of the journey alone. As much as her white partner is a bona fide ally, he is kept at a respectful distance while she single-handedly explores her Black identity.

After learning her native dance, witnessing the pastimes of Tiwi women, and tracking down her mother and grandmother in an emotional reunion, the woman Ned eventually marries is all the more whole.

Despite finding herself, Lauren was never exactly lost, as her trio of aboriginal 'sister-friends' kept her grounded. Before enjoying hen-do dance routines to Janet Jackson's 'Escapade', we learn the Tiwi word for penis, while they shrug off the fact they couldn't track down any Black phallic straws.

There are provocations here for any woman who's about to enter wedlock, especially those in an interracial relationship. How much of our culture are we really in tune with? And will our future spouse embrace the parts of our heritage that make us who we are? In Miranda's Lauren (and her divine aboriginal-print wedding dress), we see it's not only possible, but all the more beautiful for it.

OTHER ROMCOMS TO BINGE:

ALI'S WEDDING (2017)
Against the rising tide of 2018's islamophobia, Australia's first Muslim romcom helped lighten the mood.

SAVING FACE (2004)
An endearing lesbian romance that sees two Chinese-American women both embrace and break through their cultural expectations.

REMINDED WOMEN THAT 30 IS STILL YOUNG

SOMEONE GREAT

DIRECTOR: Jennifer Kaytin Robinson
WRITER: Jennifer Kaytin Robinson
YEAR: 2019

Someone Great is many things. A time capsule of millennial culture, an ode to female friendship and an example of a woman choosing her future career over a future husband. But what really fluffs the 'feminist' branded pillows we see scattered on our protagonist's couch is the empowering message from three leading women that 30 is still young enough to be unattached.

Someone Great could easily be renamed 'Three Great Women', as this neon Netflix banger injects us into the cosmopolitan lives of Jenny, Blair and Erin. In a refreshing mix of racial backgrounds (the pride from Jenny's 'Latina AF' T-shirt radiates) and sexual orientations (although, as Erin points out, 'kindly leave your heteronormative labels in the mothertucking box'), our trio unapologetically charge through New York in a *Hangover*-style blowout, before heartbroken Jenny jets off to write for *Rolling Stone*. The source of the shatteringly raw heartbreak lies with Nate, who's decided the long-distance thing just ain't gonna work.

While Jenny does address societal anxieties about entering her third decade ('I leave in a week and then I turn 30 and then I die probably'), it's more to do with having one last night with her friends than thinking she should stay and play wifey. We later learn that Blair has a self-assigned 'married before 30 steez' but still manages to dump her cringe-factory boyfriend who deep cleans her house. 'I thought I was going to be freaking out, and I am a little bit, but I mostly feel … amazing,' she triumphantly tells Erin.

Women have long been told that 30-something is time-bomb territory, where serious decisions about marital status and babies must be addressed. Such pressure can spawn bad decisions, when the person we're with becomes the person who'll do in order to obey the married-with-kids expectation. But in this break-up romcom from Jennifer Kaytin Robinson, who used her own break-up experience to pepper the plot, 'thirty, flirty and thriving' has never looked so contemporary. Via a non-judgemental depiction of a collective coming of age, we enjoy women on the cusp of 30 still centring having the time of their lives with their first true loves: their best friends.

OTHER ROMCOMS TO BINGE:

CELESTE AND JESSE FOREVER (2012)
If you want more salt in the wound of a devastating break-up, this one is a soothing reminder it was probably for the best.

DO REVENGE (2022)
Inspired by the most devilish high-school female-led comedies Jennifer Kaytin Robinson presents some candy-coloured revenge.

KNEW 40-YEAR-OLD BLACK WOMEN COULD BE SEXY AS HELL

THE FORTY-YEAR-OLD VERSION

DIRECTOR: Radha Blank
WRITERS: Radha Blank
YEAR: 2020

An unlikely union? Tick. A moment where they deepen their connection at their most emotionally vulnerable? Tick. A gay best friend? Thanks to Peter Kim? Huge tick. But unless you accidentally searched for the infamous *The 40-Year-Old Virgin*, you won't find this film in the romcom section of Netflix, which is both understandable and a shame.

By appreciating Radha Blank's semi-autobiographical film as a romcom, the genre benefits from a gasp of radical fresh air. Here we have an awkward, plus-size Black woman grappling with her magnetism in a genre that would have you believe Black women are invisible, sexless or too busy being angry to be interested in love.

The Forty-Year-Old-Version sees Blank as an aspirational hip-hop artist and theatre playwright trying to do more for the culture than plays about Black pain. She battles the compromises she has to make to appease white audiences while giving us a masterclass in reinvention as a gifted rapper she calls RadhaMUSPrime.

Bucking the erasure of big Black women and love, and the fetishisation of their sexuality, *The Forty-Year-Old Version* respectfully embraces Blank as a perfectly acceptable thirst trap. Her beauty is acknowledged by both her male and female students but, in an apt hip-hop meet-cute, it's 20-something producer D that makes her believe it for herself. He may be half her age, but he is her intellectual and emotional equal and deserving of their sexual encounter that has her asking, 'Are you beatboxing down there?' This same man helps her think twice about her diet drinks (because she's not totally immune to the pressures of slender norms) and gives her a leg up to the stage where she can be artistically free (but only after some mortifying flops).

Let's not get mad at *The Forty-Year-Old Version* for not conforming to a romcom category. How many people would dismiss this impeccably layered film if it was shoved into a generic corner? D's right. Radha Blank is 'interesting' and until romantic comedies are taken more seriously, she deserves to be discovered also by people who dismiss the genre as something to skip.

OTHER ROMCOMS TO BINGE:

THE PERFECT FIND (2023)
Gabrielle Union is enticing as a 40-year-old woman straddling a career comeback and a new young lover.

GIRLS TRIP (2017, SEE PAGE 170)
Not just one, but four leading Black women with more than a zest for life in their fourth decade.

WANTED MORE TO LIFE THAN BEING STUCK IN A RUT

PALM SPRINGS

DIRECTOR: Max Barbakow
WRITERS: Andy Siara, Max Barbakow
YEAR: 2020

Thanks to *Groundhog Day* and *About Time* we know too well how male protagonists use their time-hopping power. To be fair, *Palm Springs* also uses a boy-meets-time-loop scenario to get laid before fixing his demons, but in this modern romcom with a sci-fi zap, the girl gets to face her existential crisis too.

From the off, we meet Nyles, who has been stuck on repeat for God knows how long. Weddings are repetitive at the best of times, so imagine the toll it's taking on Nyles when he has to endlessly attend the wedding of someone he barely knows. But when the despondent sister of the bride, Sarah, unwittingly gets sucked into his live-die-repeat world, at least the monotony of life can be hilariously shared.

But it's not the time tunnel that unites Sarah and Nyles, it's loneliness – and underneath the mania of numerous suicide attempts, drug binges and liberal sexual escapades, they're both very lost. But while Nyles is resigned to being stuck in the mud of 9 November, Sarah careers through the stages of grief with hysterical denial, anger and depression. Acceptance, however, is one stage she refuses to swallow. Sarah will see 10 November – even if it kills her.

Learning quantum physics, as Sarah does to get them out of the rut, may oversimplify the complexity of overcoming our darkest days, but her determination not to accept this stagnant life is encouraging to anyone who feels that their existence has no meaning. At its most tender, *Palm Springs* reminds us that life does go round in circles, while giving us hope that someone might come along to help us enjoy the ride. Sarah knows that no man is an island and – determined she's going to live to see another day, with or without him – she tells him, 'I can survive without you ... but living with you will make life a little less mundane.'

Under the guise of our two cynical star-crossed lovers lies a new zest of modern romance. Life doesn't stop after a happily-ever-after wedding – it starts when you find someone to take a leap of faith into the unknown with.

OTHER ROMCOMS TO BINGE:

13 GOING ON 30 (2004, SEE PAGE 122)
For those of us that don't have a baggy of magic dust to go back and be a better ally, we'll just have to use this romcom to undo our wrongs.

MEET CUTE (2022)
A reminder to never try to 'fix' your new boyfriend, should you gain the power to go into their past.

THE PRINCESS DIARIES (2001)
For rejecting the expectations of how a woman is supposed to rule, this princess wore the crown.

GAVE LESBIANS A VERY HAPPY CHRISTMAS

HAPPIEST SEASON

DIRECTOR: Clea DuVall
WRITERS: Clea DuVall, Mary Holland
YEAR: 2020

For too long the world of romcoms has assumed gay folks hibernate for winter, or share in an agreement that Santa doesn't exist. Or if they do happen to venture out of the closet during the holidays, they function only to be the pragmatic best friend with way more taste. It's why 2020 was a landmark year for the gay community left in the romcom cold – until then the canon was bare of a mainstream Christmas romantic comedy featuring two women in love.

Squeezing together the tropes of both gay love stories and Christmas, *Happiest Season* is a tale about driving home and coming out; yet, under the twinkling chemistry of Kristen Stewart and Mackenzie Davis – and written and directed by lesbian icon Clea DuVall – we can stomach the predictability as easily as a supermarket mince pie. The film sees Abby gearing up to propose to girlfriend Harper, who's invited her home to spend Christmas with her conservative family. But a curveball comes crashing when Harper admits she's yet to come out and they have a long (and admittedly comical) week ahead of going back into the closet, in the literal and proverbial sense.

Christmas romcoms have long been as white as snow and as straight as candy canes, which makes anything different feel shiny and new. But beyond the crackle of new ground being broken (albeit dunked in romcom cheese), there's the gift of compassion for those who may be facing an annual shun from their family or to their true selves. It makes the title of the film ache with ironic melancholy, as for many it's far from the happiest time – but with the warm wisdom of John (gayer best friend Dan Levy), we're reminded that everyone's experience is different and the only thing each coming-out story has in common is a 'racing heart' before saying the words that can't be unsaid.

The heteronormative Christmas romcom has enjoyed mediocrity for years, so at last the gay community has a seat at the Christmas table, and considering we all deserve the comfort of clichés, *Happiest Season* offers equality in relishing its own version of banal. And let's not bah humbug that fuzzy happy ending, as it's far from familiar within a new canon being spun. For too long queer stories have ended in tragedy or gloom, so here's to *Happiest Season* coming out with festive cheer.

OTHER ROMCOMS TO BINGE:

SINGLE ALL THE WAY (2021)
You wait for one representational breakthrough and then two come at once. Netflix's first gay (and interracial!) Christmas romcom.

MAKE THE YULETIDE GAY (2009)
Come on. That lyric was always going to end up as the title to a straight-to-DVD low-budget gay romcom.

CENTRED THE TEENAGE LOVE OF A BLACK TRANS GIRL

ANYTHING'S POSSIBLE

DIRECTOR: Billy Porter
WRITERS: Ximena García Lecuona
YEAR: 2022

When screenwriter Ximena García Lecuona read someone's Reddit post asking what to do about their attraction to a trans girl, she was warmed by the internet's positive response. Enthusiastic replies cheered them on to just ask her out because 'who cares?' Talking to *The Black List*, García Lecuona (herself a trans woman) said '... I was desperately looking for stories where trans people were loved, were happy, successful in life, and satisfied ...' and after grabbing a pen, *Anything's Possible* was born.

This peppy Gen Z romcom tells the story of Kelsa (Eva Reign), a teenage girl who fancies dreamy Khalid. While he embodies the inspiration of this film with similar inquisitive Reddit threads about Kelsa, she tells her modest YouTube following her anxieties of the crush. She may express her concerns about 'someone not wanting to be with me because I'm trans or only wanting to be with me because I'm trans', but don't get it twisted: Kelsa's self-assured. We may learn that her name translates to 'brave' but she's the first to point out there's nothing brave about knowing exactly who you are. And with a wardrobe that subtly enjoys a pink, white and blue palette, she literally flies the trans flag with confidence and pride.

While the story at its heart is about the soar of young love, there's insight within all the relationships circling Kelsa's orbit. There's her mother's 'law of averages' rule that keeps her valid overprotectiveness in check, and a frenemy to confront when jealousy suggests Khalid is dating her for 'woke points'. But the relationship she has with herself is the most salient as she declares that her goal isn't just to survive high school, but to thrive.

Anything's Possible doesn't shy from issues that a Black trans teen may encounter. The second half brims with matters of bathroom bans, internet trolling, white feminism and TERFs, but against the glee of such a charismatic romance, it righteously positions them as unnecessary distractions to just trying to live. As we glide over the bumps along her way to Khalid's heart, Kelsa's goal is met in tandem with García Lecuona's – becoming a Black trans heroine who's happy, successful and loved.

OTHER ROMCOMS TO BINGE:

TANGERINE (2015)
Two best friends who happen to be Black trans women.

ALICE JÚNIOR (2019)
You know how cisgender people get loads of cute coming-of-age love stories? Here's a rare joy, centring a transgender girl from Brazil.

GIRL STROKE BOY (1971)
This *Guess Who's Coming to Dinner* plot comes with a Black trans woman twist.

HAD HONEST DISCUSSIONS
ABOUT LATER LIFE SEX

GOOD LUCK TO YOU, LEO GRANDE

DIRECTOR: Sophie Hyde
WRITERS: Katy Brand
YEAR: 2022

If *Pretty Woman* was the male fantasist version of a sex worker, *Good Luck to You, Leo Grande* is a woman's wet dream. Particularly, those who have never experienced an orgasm but are at least enjoying the thrill of free bus rides now they are 60.

While the feminist jury might be out on *Pretty Woman*, director Sophie Hyde's film is unanimously empowering, as it rubbishes the taboo of sex in later life. Here we follow 60-something widow Nancy (Emma Thompson), who after a lifetime of sexual dissatisfaction is nervously ticking off a list of things she thinks she should have enjoyed by now: 'Oral sex, her on top, doggy style and ... 69? Is that what you still call it?'

Stiflingly at first, the list is more a fetish for meeting standard objectives over individual sexual fulfilment, which is where Leo (Daryl McCormack) intervenes to calm her nerves. Over three hotel visits, he does more than tend to her body; he helps relax her mind to accept the pleasures she so deserves. Their sessions allow her to explore her fantasies, observing the boundaries she sets as she finds them, because she's never had the chance. Role play? No. Sex toys? Maybe.

Age aside, the hottest thing about this sexual journey is how consent acts as foreplay, as Leo gently takes on the mental effort needed to communicate needs. At each checkpoint he asks if he can kiss, stroke or simply pour her a glass of champagne, making her feel in control without taking the reins. As for that orgasm, Leo helps her remove the stigma in her desire, as anyone with that much internalized shame is never going to relax enough to climax, and as Nancy surrenders on the bed, wearing nothing but a secret smile, we know she's finally found the meaning of coming of age.

Leo shares enough insight into his experience as a sex worker to tell Nancy that his oldest client was 82, making us question Nancy's shock as we ask ourselves, well ... why not? It's here we get the newsflash that women can, and do, enjoy sex well into their mature years and the idea of sexual prime is an ageist myth.

OTHER ROMCOMS TO BINGE:

HOPE SPRINGS (2012)
Meryl Streep bangs as a woman who puts some me time into her sex life, sometimes bringing along her husband of 30 years for the ride.

LET THE SUNSHINE IN (2017)
Juliette Binoche (directed by the excellent Claire Denis) as a middle-aged woman finding a higher-class sex life.

HAROLD AND MAUDE (1971, SEE PAGE 36)
As the octogenarian icon of the romcom scene, we could all learn a thing or two from Maude, who still knows how to get her kicks.

OPENED UP THE CONVERSATION ABOUT ASSISTED MARRIAGES

WHAT'S LOVE GOT TO DO WITH IT?

DIREOTOR: Shekhar Kapur
WRITER: Jemima Khan
YEAR: 2022

Many a romcom have relied on the friction of a culture clash. While relishing the theory of opposites attract, it can also hold a mirror up to Western ignorance. *What's Love Got to Do with It?* explores our understanding of how arranged – sorry, assisted – marriages work and how choice is still paramount on who they marry (or divorce).

Childhood friends Zoe and Kazim live next door but are a continent apart. He's a Pakistani Muslim and she's as white as a microwave pack of rice. When Kaz tells Zoe that his parents are finding him a wife, curious (and heartbroken) she asks, 'What about love?' While explaining that 'it's just a different way of getting there', he agrees to be the subject of her documentary *Love Contractually* to help her understand.

Borrowing familiar sauce from *When Harry Met Sally,* South Asian couples address the camera on how their relationships began. Here we learn how arranged marriages have evolved, providing insight into how they often conveniently lead to love.

Despite flinging around stats like 'only 6 per cent of assisted marriages end in divorce', writer Jemima Khan is careful not to over-romanticize this cultural norm. Embedded in the dialogue and the genuinely hilarious script (indebted to Emma Thompson as Zoe's mum and Asim Chaudhry as 'Mo the Matchmaker'), topics of colourism provide darker food for thought. But it's Kaz's Pakistani bride Maymouna who blasts open some bias when her quiet, suppressed demeanour flips to someone with sass. And when Zoe's documentary is accused of a 'white gaze' (something this film goes to lengths to avoid), it also becomes Maymouna's catalyst to call the wedding off.

What's Love Got to Do with It? chews on some meaty provocation. Can love 'simmer first and then boil'? And is involving your parents 'just a 3D version of halal Tinder'? Also, by going on blind dates (as Zoe's mum instigates) and swiping through dating apps, are assisted relationships something we're all doing anyway?

Using the featherweight power of a mainstream romcom, Khan and Kapur have highlighted an often-misunderstood culture with enough shine to reflect its pros and cons. While successful arrangements can indeed lead to love, if it doesn't work out, there's always the person next door.

OTHER ROMCOMS TO BINGE:

BRIDE & PREJUDICE (2004)
Jane Austen – desi-style – reminding us that white women in the eighteenth century have always been into marrying off their kids.

STAND UP FOR LOVE (2017)
The family are arranging the marriage, can they also sort out the groom's erectile dysfunction? Hilariously (and progressively), they try.

DIDN'T WHITEWASH THE CITY

RYE LANE

DIRECTOR: Raine Allen-Miller
WRITERS: Nathan Bryon, Tom Melia
YEAR: 2023

If the city is a third character in a movie, *Rye Lane's* director Raine Allen-Miller has made a throuple with Yas, Dom and South London. In a genre that routinely throws shade on the visibility of Black people, *Rye Lane* has shown just how embedded Black culture is in the capital.

Thanks to her wide-angle lens, Allen-Miller wraps her arms around the city she loves, cramming in the glorious idiosyncrasies of a space that has long benefitted from the arrival of immigrant communities. The ones who injected the NHS with nurses, helped rebuild Britain after the Second World War and lubricated London's stiff dance floors with rhythm and blues.

As we watch the romance unfurl between Yas and Dom, *Rye Lane* raises a toast to the many threads Black culture has woven into the fabric of the UK. From the food and fabric stalls standing proud in the face of gentrification, to the adorable walking-and-talking scenes across Windrush Square.

Aside from the intrinsic sense of place, *Rye Lane* gifts us Yas (Vivian Oparah), the infectious, screwball character who is one half of our delightful couple, who also happen to be Black. A Black romance that's not about their struggle is about as rare as an affordable flat in Brixton, and apart from a genius cameo by Colin Firth at a 'Love Guac'tually' burrito stall, we see nothing but Black and brown angles within hilariously pointy love triangles.

This representation is important. Through the filter of Richard Curtis' romcoms that twinkle as white as snow, the UK appears bereft of people of colour – let alone any in love or in leading roles. *Rye Lane* helps skew that view with a triumphant lick of luminosity and, despite being such a quintessential South London film, it cuddles up to the universal story of finding love in a hopeless place (sobbing in a unisex toilet cubicle, to be exact).

OTHER ROMCOMS TO BINGE:

BEEN SO LONG (2018)
A breakthrough Black British romance complete with spontaneous song and dance. Michaela Coel makes sparks fly.

BOOMERANG (1992, SEE PAGE 58)
The biggest budget Black romcom of its time, which painted New York as so Black that white critics actually took issue with its 'improbably glamorous corporate universe'.

BABYMOTHER (1998)
Often claimed as the first Black British musical, this celebration of dancehall culture uses an authentic South London stage for its mic-battle romance.

TOOK THE BATTLE OF THE SEXES TO A WHOLE NEW LEVEL

BARBIE

DIRECTOR: Greta Gerwig
WRITERS: Greta Gerwig, Noah Baumbach
YEAR: 2023

Behold Romcom Barbie, whose quest to the Real World reimagined the battle of the sexes. And then there's Ken. Who, contrary to the marketing, is more than 'just Ken', as he joins Barbie on an existential road trip that trashes gender norms.

Romantic comedies have forever indulged us with women vs men, as crystallized so superbly in *When Harry Met Sally*. It's a tried-and-tested formula that has buoyed the genre for years, but in acknowledging the fact that reinforcing binaries is archaic, how will the romcom evolve without its key stock?

This is where pop culture's most famous couple step in to rewrite the rules, by going from stiletto-heel to flat Birkenstock and upending feminine ideals. And after Ken's discovery, and then rejection, of this unearned power called patriarchy, he presents the concept as destructive for himself and his fellow Kens.

In this observed twist on the battle of the sexes, the biggest war we see is with gender itself. In a world of living up to the demands of femininity and masculinity, we see burnouts from trying to conform. Of course, this gets complicated, considering Barbie dolls haven't helped, but the intent of the product had its heart in the right place. By doing away with the baby dolls that reared girls to be mothers, the playground of womanhood was now at their feet: Barbie had her own home, smart friends and over 150 careers; yet, in an eerie parallel of the treatment of women, we focus on her looks rather than what she's achieved.

As for relationship goals we may have of Barbie and Ken, they become more aspirational after they split. In a mature separation for a duo who were designed to be together, Barbie reminds Ken that he's more than just someone's girlfriend and there's more to life than 'beach'.

Despite being marketed as a chick flick on steroids, Barbie riffs on the experience of both women and men, but while the latter are emancipated by rejecting toxic masculinity, women are shown compassion in understanding how hard it is to just exist. It's this level of insight we should want from our romcoms, honestly portraying the exhaustion of living up to gender norms. In removing the expectations of what those ideals look like, we'll have more time on our hands to argue about what romcom to watch next.

OTHER ROMCOMS TO BINGE:

WHEN HARRY MET SALLY (1989, SEE PAGE 54)
To revisit one of the original and best battle-of-the-sexes romcoms.

DON JON (2013)
Another Barbie (but this one's called Barbara and is played by Scarlett Johannson) waking another man up from his toxic-masculinity nightmare.

INDEX OF FILMS

GENERAL INDEX

BIOGRAPHIES

ABOUT THE AUTHOR

Corrina Antrobus is a film critic whose life's
work has been dedicated to championing
underrepresented groups in cinema. In 2014
she founded London's popular feminist film
festival The Bechdel Test Fest – an ongoing
celebration of films that pass the Bechdel
Test, also known as the Wallace-Bechdel
Test. The festival ran for seven years and
hosted screenings, talks, created zines and
produced the Who Is She podcast in 2019.
Corrina has reviewed films for *Empire*
magazine, *Rolling Stone*, BBC, *Total Film*,
Huffington Post and was the resident host
for Channel 4's Sunday Brunch. In 2020
Corrina wrote and voiced a documentary
on Ava DuVernay for BBC's Inside Cinema,

was nominated for a Screen Rising Star Award in 2019 and was awarded a Women in
Hollywood Trailblazer award in 2017. She has worked in film marketing for Virgin Movies,
film distribution for Picturehouse Entertainment and now works as a writer, Q&A host,
a culture lead for her home town of Hackney and is a full time mother.

ABOUT THE ILLUSTRATOR

Lily O'Farrell is a feminist writer and cartoonist from London, in 2018 she started
@vulgadrawings. She published her first book *Kyle Theory* with The Indigo Press in 2021,
and currently has a documentary podcast series called No Worries If Not! covering
women and internet culture.

ACKNOWLEDGEMENTS

Big love to the critics, programmers and fellow film lovers who answered the call 'what's your favourite feminist romcom?' Including Christina Newland, Pamela Huchinson, Hannah Flint, Mike McCahill, Leigh Singer, Fong Chau, Dan Castella, Sam Clements, Paul Ridd, *Reclaim The Frame's* Melanie Iredale, *Women Over 50 Film Festival's* Nuala O'Sullivan, *We Are Parable's* Anthony and Teanne Andrews and the endless well of knowledge, wisdom and comic relief that is 'Woo Hoo'. My Bechdel Test Fest die-hards Beth Webb, Caitlin Quinlan and Stephanie Watts where in another life (or economic climate) we'd be screening the hell out of all these films (or at least *Moonstruck* again). Thank you to Alice Guilluy and Tamar Jeffers McDonald for all your extensive romcom research at an intimidatingly intelligent level. I learned so much. To anyone who's ever hosted a romcom podcast - I've probably found you. To the muscles behind this book at Quarto; Andrew Roff and Laura Bulbeck - well, that conversation about romcoms escalated! Thank you for finding me. Beth Free, thank you for your wonderful design work. Immense gratitude to Lily O'Farrell for bringing this to life with such visionary talent.

To my beautiful Bitches, with you as my cheerleaders anything is possible. To my little village; Ray, Tab, Ira, Graham and Ellie and matriarchs Rosie and Kim who gave me space to watch, read, write and bang my head against a wall while I cashed in babysitting cheques, this exists because of you. And to new mothers who still want to do that thing that makes you feel fulfilled - you can. It just takes a different route.

To Toby. I'm just a girl, standing in front of a boy, asking him to still love her even though she's filled the house with romcom DVDs. Thank you for your patience and belief in me. You and OAK are everything.

Quarto

First published in 2024 by White Lion Publishing,
an imprint of The Quarto Group.
One Triptych Place, London, SE1 9SH,
United Kingdom
T (0)20 7700 9000
www.Quarto.com

A catalogue record for this book is available from the British Library.

ISBN 978-0-7112-9070-9
Ebook ISBN 978-0-7112-9071-6

10 9 8 7 6 5 4 3 2 1

Cover Design and Illustration; Internal Design: Beth Free, Studio Nic&Lou
Publisher: Jessica Axe
Commissioning Editor: Andrew Roff
Editorial Director: Jennifer Barr
Senior Editor: Laura Bulbeck
Editorial Assistant: Izzy Toner
Senior Designer: Renata Latipova
Production Controller: Rohana Yusof

Printed in China